BRAN NUE DAE

A musical journey

Jimmy Chi

and

Kuckles

Bran Nue Dae premiered at the Perth International Arts Festival in 1990 to packed houses and standing ovations. National tours followed, and *Bran Nue Dae* was celebrated as one of Australia's most successful musicals. In 2020, *Bran Nue Dae* was remounted by Opera Australia. However, a proposed national tour was cut short by the COVID-19 pandemic.

Jimmy Chi and Kuckles

Jimmy Chi (1948–2017) was born in Broome to a father of Chinese and Japanese descent. His mother was the daughter of a Bard woman from the Dampier Peninsula and a Scottish station manager. Jimmy and his colleagues won numerous awards for *Bran Nue Dae*, including the Sidney Myer Performing Arts Award and a Certificate of Commendation in the 1991 Human Rights Awards.

Kuckles was formed in the early 1980s when Broome musicians Jimmy Chi, Stephen Pigram, Michael Mavromatis (Manolis), Garry Gower and Patrick Bin Amat attended the Centre for Aboriginal Studies in Music (CASM) in Adelaide. In 1981 they released 'Milliya Rumurra', their best-known recording, which means 'brand new day' in the Yawuru language. Their distinctive sound incorporated Bard/Bardi language with acoustic calypso and electric reggae-rock styles. The original band members, their children and grandchildren have performed in all productions of the stage play of *Bran Nue Dae*.

This edition is a reproduction of the original book published in 1991.
We respectfully caution Aboriginal and Torres Strait Islander readers that this book contains images and names of people who have passed away.

Contents

Chorus, 'On the way to a Bran Nue Dae', Perth Festival, March 1990, premiere season.

Introduction

Welcome to the world of *Bran Nue Dae*. The setting is Sun Pictures in Broome, a site of the sacred and profane, where they've been showing movies for over 80 years — and where, they say, most of the town's love stories began. Some things never change. Or is it as another song says: 'The world keeps on turning and will never be the same?'

This is a story of how someone found his uncle and a whole lot more besides. Since white settlement of the country, Australians have looked on while bureacracy ripped, religioned, cajoled and legislated Black children away from their families, mothers from their children, fathers from their roles. This was called 'assimilation'. If it had succeeded a culture would be extinct, and a unique identity lost. Of course it did not succeed, and not just because the policy was a half-baked shambles from the start, a bureaucrat's persistent dream, a blind nation's backdoor nightmare. Assimilation could never have succeeded, and this musical tells us why. Australia has a Black soul.

Fifteen years ago, give or take, the idea of a musical about a journey to consciousness was born in a young man's brain, but so were a million ideas in just as many brains. This idea lived because the young man in question had taken a walloping from his experiences of dislocation and imposed aspirations. He also grew up through the 1960s, which may have had something to do with it. Jimmy Chi was not an exceptional musician. He was self-taught, which in his crowd was usual. In a town of songwriters, he had a special gift for melody and spellbinding performance. At parties he would sing a piece, sometimes sitting on the grass, 'Is You Mah Baby?' and he would shake, and rattle, and roll the intellect — no one could sing it like him and the word virtuoso came to mind. The idea had begun to take shape in songs.

These songs were first performed by Kuckles, the Broome band that composed them in the way groups do: for gigs in bars and parties, at early morning beaches and on the road. Kuckles was a kind of rambunctious nursery, five men making music without thinking that one day the world might hear their work as a spiritual/rock/reggae opera. That destiny is now cast, and what unfolds may give us cause to wonder. Critics will make their judgement of this play, with its sparkling lines, rich music and the orbital engine of its plot, but we can say now: it is a landmark work. As theatre director Brian Syron pointed out after the early trial of a few scenes in Sydney: 'The people need this.'

Sun Pictures, Broome, circa 1920.

Kuckles was a band defying the odds. Broome is such a long way from anywhere that it might as well be nowhere, which is perhaps a good starting point for surprises. But far though it may be, the old pearling port has a musical tradition as potent as the brews and as heady as the brawls of its past, with country music as deliciously present in parody — 'Time Will Heal' — as in comedy — 'Seeds That You Might Sow' — as well as in gospel, soul, torch, spoof, satire and passion. It is the music of a four-generation subculture that had a language and fun all its own: weekend fishing, a verandah, a guitar that had first to be mastered — lessons with a record scratched by repetition and a spinifex needle — an evening stroll or making love, not always with official blessing, or a visit to Sun Pictures and a seat in a segregated audience.

The old cinema with its ageing screen is still there. *Solid*, they say of this building. Just as well, for something cyclonic hit out of season, in September 1990, when volunteer carpenters and donated front-end loaders descended to make a jetty stage and tidal pools where the front row of canvas seats had once wriggled to impatient bottoms. With scaffold seating erected to accommodate a week of sellout houses, *Bran Nue Dae* played to its home town. 'Yeah, I'm a man now,' says Willie, in jail — and he is a Royal Commission in five words. They wept, laughed and anticipated lines, the songs scored in their own hearts. A thrilled audience stood to applaud, whistle and sing, night after night. But there is more to this story.

In 1986 the musical was still just an idea and a few songs. Enter the Aboriginal Writers, Oral Literature and Dramatists Association (AWOLDA). They put the idea through a staging workshop in Perth, where playright and poet Jack Davis gave advice. Jimmy Chi returned to Broome encouraged, but it was Marita Darcy who drove the tardy genius to get his musical down. The result of their interaction was a first draft. Some scenes were still in outline and the structure was picaresque but it suggested a powerful drama — and it was written. Magabala Books had been recently started in Broome. *Just in time*, you might say. The brave new Aboriginal publishing house was on hand to prepare a bright new work for presentation to theatre producers.

The interest that followed was not overwhelming but it was stimulating enough to keep *Bran Nue Dae* on course. This nurture at arm's length came happily from Robyn Kershaw and then Duncan Ord of Perth's Black Swan Theatre Company and Tasmania's Salamanca Theatre, and closer up with a solid embrace from the Aboriginal National Theatre Trust (ANTT), which flew Jimmy Chi to Sydney in January 1989 to workshop some scenes and songs, with help from the Aboriginal Arts Board of the Australia Council.

Kuckles' manager Peter Strain found finance for further development, script editing and music transcription. The work was becoming known. Some realised that a theatrical coup was waiting for a company daring enough to show faith. Philip Parsons of Currency Press has watched over the birth of more Australian theatre than there are wharves to Sydney Harbour. On reading the text, listening to the demo tapes and hearing Chi himself delivering those pungent lines of dialogue, he was moved. 'This is it. The Australian musical we've all been waiting for. It has everything, it must be done.'

Back home, they needed no convincing. Having grown up with Chi, they knew this to be an enterprise of great pith and moment. They formed a working group led by Peter Yu, created Bran Nue Dae Productions, and appointed Chris McGuigan executive producer. He and Yu approached Andrew Ross to direct, impressed by his sensitive work on the plays of Jack Davis. The Black Swan Theatre Company had agreed to put on the show.

The redrafted script was handed to Ross on a sunny day in Melbourne, which had to be propitious. With it came a challenging task. *Bran Nue Dae* would premiere at the Festival of Perth in February 1990. It would have six weeks to prepare in Broome, using a cast mainly of local actors but with professionals brought in for the leading roles. There would be just two weeks further rehearsal in Perth before the opening at the Octagon Theatre. Ross arrived in Broome having already devised vital changes to make the script work on stage. Scenes were simplified, dialogue woven through songs. In the sweat of tropical January heat, in an unlined iron shed in Broome, helped by buckets of iced water and inspiring sunsets, thirteen actors, director Ross and choreographer Michael Leslie put it all together, with those Kuckles musicians once again. The show was the hit of the festival. It went on to a second production, and after singing and dancing its way through the north-west, toured interstate with mounting success. One of those eleven first tour venues was the school lawn at Kalumburu. Flying by five light planes over the awesome Mitchell Plateau to the furthest of places, *Bran Nue Dae* returned to its roots in an Aboriginal community, playing to an audience on the grass, from a stage marked by a ring of flour. A self-raising musical, or miracle.

So much for beginnings. *Bran Nue Dae* is made to travel. It has healing, happy and zestful work to do. It is a suitcase stuffed with magnificent songs. It is a love letter, like Little Abby's, to a wiser present; a musical that will continue to win over audiences long after recession, athletic interest rates, AIDS and ozone holes are, we hope, consigned to a past century. I can't think of a better anthem to take us into the next than 'Child of Glory' or 'Everybody Looking for Kuckle', 'Sweet Sister' or 'Listen to the News', 'Marijuana Annie' or the title song itself. They will be singing these songs on their way to liberation in South Africa, they will sing them for warmth in Russian winters and with astounded recognition in Berlin. Even Nue Yorkers will feel that way again. World, welcome to *Bran Nue Da*e.

Peter Bibby, Broome, 1991

The author in rehearsal, Broome, January 1990.

Sun Pictures, Broome, September, 1990.

Act One

Sun Pictures, Broome

Two rows of deckchairs face one another across the forestage. Streeter's Jetty projects towards the audience, with a pool of water on either side. On the jetty are small railway lines. There is sand and coloured Broome rocks. In the back the bare sand of Kennedy Hill, making three levels of stage. The Sun Pictures movie screen is the backdrop.

[SALLY ANNE *enters chewing a Cherry Ripe chocolate bar. Other members of the chorus —* BERNADETTE, LUCY, RITA, TONI, FRANCES *— enter behind and take seats on either side.*]

SALLY ANNE — You want some? [*Offering Cherry Ripe.*]

BERNADETTE — No, go away Sally Anne.

[SALLY ANNE *walks over to the other row of deckchairs.*]

FRANCES — There your mummy there.

SALLY ANNE — Where's my mummy?

[WILLIE *and* ROSIE *enter, to sit on opposite sides.* CHARLIE *enters stage left with soiled pants pulled up high and cracked glasses, reading a PIX magazine.*]

SALLY ANNE — Can I sit down here?

[SALLY ANNE *plumps herself down between* WILLIE *and the rest. This throws* WILLIE *off his end of the deckchair row.* LITTLE ABBY *and* PETER *enter.*]

PETER — Hey boy, he tonguing for you.

LITTLE ABBY — Munga dog.

[*Everyone laughs.* LUCY *calls across.*]

LUCY — Hey Rosie, he wanna sit wit you!

(Opposite) Tadpole (Ernie Dingo), Marijuana Annie (Lynda Nutter) and chorus, Perth.

ROSIE Who?

LUCY Willie.

ROSIE He stalebait.

SALLY ANNE He deadly boy. He come from Lombadina.

BERNADETTE He bin Perth for schooling, Rossmoyne.

RITA That Father Benedictus.

OTHERS And he going back too.

[ROSIE *works her way in embarrassment to centre stage.*]

ALL He wanna sit wit you at Sun Pictures.

[WILLIE *runs to* ROSIE *at base of the jetty as the movie begins with the leader countdown 10 to 1, followed by 'God Save the Queen' with Elizabeth II on a horse. The queen's head goes off the screen.* WILLIE *and* ROSIE *are transported into the movie.* CHORUS *exits.*]

ROSIE What, Willie?

[*Song: 'Light a Light'*]

WILLIE *Hey girl, you know I've been a dreamer*
following dreams I've dreamed on my own.
Though the dreams are the dreams that sustain me,
I'm tired of dreaming alone.

[CHORUS *re-enters from stage right bearing lighted candles.*]

CHORUS *Light a light, leave it in the window,*
I'm comin' back, back home to you.
Light a light, leave it in the window
I'll be comin' back home.

There are times when I'm feelin' so fearful
times when I'm cut up and crying inside,
those times that find me always remind me
of hoping to find you here by my side.

Light a light, leave it in the window,
I'm comin' back, back home to you.
Light a light, leave it in the window,
I'll be comin' back home.

Light a light, leave it in the window,
I'm comin' back, back home to you.
Light a light, leave it in the window,
I'll be comin' back home
I'll be comin' back home.

[*A big refrigerator is wheeled on, with candle holders all around it.* CHORUS *place their candles in the holders.* ROSIE *gives* WILLIE *a friendly glance and wave, and leaves him.*]

Rohanna Angus and John Moore in rehearsal, Canberra.

Rossmoyne Pallottine Aboriginal Hostel

[*There is an explosion and* BENEDICTUS *appears in a cloud of smoke, wearing a black cassock embroidered with Cherry Ripe bars and with a tall mitre and huge crook with a large hook. He wears shoulder pads and built-up shoes, making him larger than life.*]

BENEDICTUS [*German accent.*] Ah so, Villie! Come een fellow!! Velkom to der city. How are you, my leedle flend?

WILLIE Gud, fada.

BENEDICTUS So fellow, vot haff you been doing? Did you catch any fish vile avay on holidays?

WILLIE No fada.

BENEDICTUS So fellow you must inspect every awailable vacancy at Clontarf to become a successful indaweedal.

WILLIE Yes fada.

BENEDICTUS Villie Villie, ven Joshua valked around
Jericho, he did so at the Lord's kommand.
You can't get to heaven if you don't go to the
sacraments and just sprinkle your arse vit holy vater!

WILLIE Yes fada.

BENEDICTUS Villie, you can go fort and help your people — dey are crying in dere vildemess. You haff so much to gif the vorld! So my leedle flend enjoy your stay wit derfellows; den you can knuckle down to some serious study! Now go —

[WILLIE *is half way off.*]

Ah Villie!
Vill you not be one of my leedle altar boys tomorrow?

WILLIE Okay fada Benedictus. See you fada.

[*Light dims on* BENEDICTUS. *Light comes up on the fridge where* WILLIE *is leading a raid on the tuckshop with* PETER, DARRYL *and* LITTLE ABBY.]

WILLIE Bro — no one coming!

LITTLE ABBY Nuh Benny's done his rounds.

[WILLIE *breaks into the tuckshop and opens the fridge, revealing Cherry Ripes and Cokes, etc.*]

ALL [*Exclaiming*] Wahh ...!!

[WILLIE *takes out a little black book, pretends to be taking orders.*]

WILLIE What you want bro?

Willie (John Moore) and chorus (Jimmy Edgar, Ricky Haji Noor, Brian Saaban, Michael Leslie and Cecilia Dann), Canberra.

PETER Coke-coke! Cherry Ripe too, bro!
— and Roasted Peanuts!

ROB What you doing bro?

WILLIE Itemising ewery awailable confection unt
bewerage purchase, bro.

PETER You think yourself accountant?

WILLIE Yeah, like St Peter, bro. [*They laugh.*]

DARRYL Is Benny looking?

WILLIE Uh — Benny!

[WILLIE *runs up the hill and looks to stage right and comes back.*]

WILLIE No.

Andrew Ross directing, with John Moore as Willie, in rehearsal, Canberra.

[*The boys stuff their shirts as they leave the tuckshop, move to the side and sit down for a feast.*]

Yah it is gut to eat at der Lord's table. First ve haff made un inwentory ov der spoils. [*He holds the black book up.*]

Den ve haff to partake of der fruits ov our labours. Thank you Lord —

ALL Thank you Lord!

PETER Und dis is for all der starfing kids in der vorld — [*He bites into a Cherry Ripe bar.*]

DARRYL Like us ay bro, us blackies starving.

ROB Yeah bro.

WILLIE Und den der liquid refreshments
to make it taste efen bedder!

ALL Ya, ya

[*There is the tinkling of a bell.* DARRYL *runs up the hill and whistles a warning.*]

DARRYL Benny, Benny comin —

[WILLIE *drops the black book and* LITTLE ABBY *drops an unfinished note to his girlfriend in the confusion of clearing up bottles and wrappers.*]

[*To the strains of the song 'Calling in the Name',* BENEDICTUS *paces on in stately fashion, passing near the black book and then over it. He leads them on like the pied piper, singing stoutly with crook and mitre. The congregation fans out on either side of stage,* BENEDICTUS *in the centre with* WILLIE *on the left and* DARRYL *on the right, staggering under the weight of the missal.*]

CONGREGATION

Hey listen people
He is calling in the name
He is shattering the idols
Which He scatters on the plain
He is washing all the nations
In a spiritual refrain
And the world keeps on turning
And will never be the same.

[*Kids make fun of* BENEDICTUS *behind his back.*]

There's a new day dawning
And it's wiping out the tears
With the task unfolding
With the passing of the years.
Take the word upon you
To the corners of the world
Lead the people into battle
With his banners all unfurled.

[*Kids dart out, lift and look under his cloak and dart back.*]

See the light arising
From the east unto the west
Seeing all the nations being put unto the test.
There's no time to falter, we all have to be refined
Purged of all the coarseness
And remade to his design.

BENEDICTUS Dere are many evils in der vorld today.

[*The angelus is rung.*]

Countless innumerable abominations to der Lord. However, for now let us just talk about theft und pillage. Und der sins ov der flesh.

Chorus (Michael Leslie, Rohanna Angus, Della Morrison, Josephine Lawford), Kalumburu.

Willie (John Moore), chorus and Benedictus (Robert Faggetter) performing 'Nothing I Would Rather Be,' Adelaide.

[*Kids make fun of the sermon, pick their noses and gesticulate.* DARRYL *swings the smoking thurible between his legs.*]

My greatest desire is to see der native
people be edercarted und trained in der
skills ov der modern vorld. To become
citerzens ov dis country dat is truly deres.
Ve haff to show luff to dese children so dat
dey can indeed fulfil der motto:
Lux in tenebris — light in der darkness!

[*The angelus is rung.* BENEDICTUS *stares meaningfully at* WILLIE. *He closes with benediction.*]

[*Nasal.*] The Lord be wif you.

CONGREGATION

[*Nasal.*] And also wif you.

[*The altar boys file past for the last rousing chorus of 'Calling in the Name'.* BENEDICTUS *begins swatting his altar boys, whacking each on the hand with a slapstick.*]

CONGREGATION

See the light arising
From the east unto the west
Seeing all the nations being put unto the test.
There's no time to falter, we all have to be refined
Purged of all the coarseness
And remade to his design.
Hey listen people
He is calling in the name.

[*A break in the music.* WILLIE *pulls his hands away to avoid the whack.*]

BENEDICTUS By hook or by crook I vill vack you!!

[*He whacks* WILLIE *on the behind.*]

Michelle Torres-Hill, Della Morrison, John Moore and Alan Charlton in rehearsal, first production, Broome.

WILLIE Oohh —

CONGREGATION

He is shattering the idols
Which He scatters on the plain
He is washing all the nations
In a spiritual refrain
And the world keeps on turning
And will never be the same.

[CHORUS *as children take up positions either side in the Sun Pictures deck chairs.*]

BENEDICTUS [*Exhausted.*] Vell vorking boys und schoolies ve vould like to velcome our representatives at Clontarf. Villie back home for turd Sunday as you all know.

And ve haff some messages from der little angels ... Ve need someone to select a message. Abby vill you not come up?

[*Frighteened,* LITTLE ABBY *gets up from far right stage and moves to BENEDICTUS' side, centre stage, while the kids sing out.*]

CHORUS Yoh yoh Abby. [*Pointing.*] Leg leg —

[LITTLE ABBY*'s right leg is shaking uncontrollably.* BENEDICTUS *points with his crook to* LITTLE ABBY*'s love note, which he had dropped during the tuckshop raid. It is right at his feet.* LITTLE ABBY *picks it up and* BENEDICTUS *hooks him round the neck and pulls him up close. He takes the note and reads it to assembly.*]

BENEDICTUS 'Hey boy you make me itchy
I'm alvay tonguing for you!'

[LITTLE ABBY *expects the worst but* BENEDICTUS *lets him off, points him back to his seat.* BENEDICTUS *glances severely at* WILLIE.]

Villy! Vill you not come up
und see vat ve haft?

[*Drum roll à la 'Madame Guillotine' —* WILLIE *approaches* BENEDICTUS, *who points with his crook to the black book on the floor.* WILLIE *picks it up.* BENEDICTUS *then hooks him round the neck and draws him close up.* BENEDICTUS *takes the book.*]

Ah a present for der good fada. A diary!
Vat haff ve now? [*Reads entries.*]
Saturday 24th Nowember, 4 bottle Coke (large)
10 pkts Cherry Ripe! 20 pkts Roasted Peanuts
Der list ... ah der list of omissions!

Der list goes on und on! Villy you are a rotten abble in der barrel. You are a blot on der mission and a stain on der celebration of life.

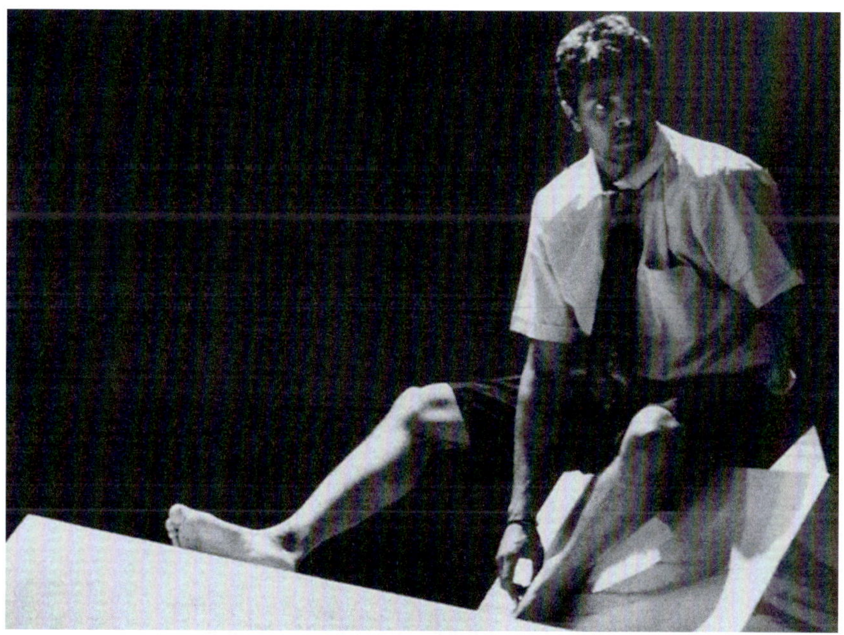

Willie (John Moore), Perth.

[*Ominous strains as* BENEDICTUS *hooks him with the crook, moving him forward and back.*]

Stupid kit you are an abomination to der
Lord. You are sex und drugs in Chinatown,
drinking in der park, looking up der girlies
dresses und creeping in der dark.

WILLIE No fada.

[*Boys cheer.* BENEDICTUS *thinks he is receiving approval from them and he sets* WILLIE *down.*]

BENEDICTUS You vill never change —
You are zer leedle Hitler!
You are leading der boys astray.
Ve haff no rooms for failures —
or ve vant is sugcess!

Willie (John Moore) collared by Benedictus (Robert Faggetter), Adelaide Festival Centre.

CHORUS Oooohhhh ...

[BENEDICTUS, *with a sweep of the crook, hurls* WILLIE *to the floor. For a moment he is motionless. The* CHORUS *cheers as he recovers and rises to sing defiantly.*]

[*Song: 'Nothing I Would Rather Be'*]

WILLIE
There's nothing I would rather be
than to be an Aborigine
and watch you take my precious land away.
For nothing gives me greater joy than to
watch you fill each girl and boy
with superficial existential shit.

[CHORUS *dance on from the side.*]

CHORUS
Now you may think I'm cheeky
but I'd be satisfied
to rebuild your convict ships
and sail you on the tide.

WILLIE
I love the way you give me God
and of course the mining board
for this of course I thank the lord each day.
I'm glad you say that land rights wrong
then you should go where you belong
and leave me to just keep on keeping on.

WILLIE and CHORUS
Now you may think I'm cheeky
but I'd be satisfied,
to rebuild your convict ships
and sail you on the tide.

WILLIE
There's nothing I would rather be
than to be an Aborigine
and dream of just what heaven must be like,
where moth and rust do not corrupt

when I die I know I'll be going up,
cos you know that I've had my hell on earth.

CHORUS *God gave us ten commandments,*
ve know ve are informed.

BENEDICTUS [*Slowly, ominous strains.*]
Judgement day is coming,
ve always being va-aa-rrrned.

[*On the back projection is Michaelangelo's 'Creation of Adam.'* WILLIE *and* BENEDICTUS *almost touch fingers.* WILLIE *is thrown back from the contact.*]

CHORUS *There's nothing I would rather be*
than to be an Aborigine
and watch you take my precious land away.
No no no no —
And watch you take my precious land away.

BENEDICTUS Ohhhhh no!

[CHORUS *of children exits.*]

By hook or by crook I vill vack you to sort
out dis sordid mess. Clear out of Der House
of Der Lord, Der Temple of Der Soul.
Clear out! Go!!
Back vhere you came from, go!!!

[*A scared* WILLIE *exits as if expelled from the Garden of Eden: out of one life and into another.*]

WILLIE No faaada!

Tadpole (Steven Albert) in second production, Canberra.

City park at night

[TADPOLE *enters from stage right and lights fire.* CHORUS *of fringe dwellers enters wearing blankets.*]

[*Song: 'Longway Away From My Country'*]

TADPOLE *I'm a longway away from my country,*
It's a long time since I've reappeared.
It's the feeling I feel
When you're close on the wheel
And I'm missing the touch of your hand.

It's no good this feeling of sorrow,
Just go out and face it alone
And I'm waiting tonight,
A watch in the night
And thinking of just going home.

[WILLIE *walks on in a desolate mood, much the worse for wear. He is attracted by the singing and the company but hesitates, unfamiliar with that lifestyle, and disturbed to find himself a part of it.*]

Park chorus (Josephine Lawford, Rohanna Angus, Sylvia Clarke, Rasidah Bin Omar and Cecilia Dann), Canberra.

[*There is some movement among the people: a woman getting up, someone stirring the fire, some drinking, handing a flagon around, touching and sharing during the song.* TADPOLE *notices* WILLIE.]

TADPOLE Hey boy where you bin come from?
What you name?

[WILLIE *steps over to the campfire.*]

WILLIE Father bin kick me out. I got nowhere to stay I wanna go home to Broome.

[WILLIE *sits dejected, cross legged, head in hands, at a loss.*]

TADPOLE I come from Broome too but you still never tell me your name yet.

WILLIE My name William Johnson.

TADPOLE Yeah eh! You know what? My name ... my name Steven Johnson. But I'm your uncle, Uncle Tadpole! I bin away for 20 years now.

I bin drovin' I bin drinkin' I bin Christian,
I bin everything; but now its time
I gotta go home before I die.
I gotta see old people.

CHORUS *So come on you restless young riders,*
Come on you young roving kinds.
Unless you're prepared
It's not like you've heard,
Cos you'll find that you'll run out of time.

[WILLIE, *embarrassed by* TADPOLE, *moves away, afraid of throwing in his lot with him and ending up like him.* TADPOLE *shuffles and swings over to* WILLIE.]

TADPOLE Come on we better piss off eh!
Come on let's go walking down this road
and fuckin' find a place to go home, c'mon.
Yeah my boy, c'mon hurry up, let's go home.
We got no time to muck around!
You know what! Your mother is my uncle brother and that's my brother but this is my sister so he call you uncle. That's how come I'm your sister brother and I'm your uncle and so I'm your uncle, OKAY!?

WILLIE Yeah Uncle. But who is my daddy?

TADPOLE What they bin doing to you my boy, they bin hit you!

WILLIE Yeah fada bin hit me. They bin chuck me out from mission.

TADPOLE How come? What you bin doing?

WILLIE Uh I bin ... uh I bin trying to grab some tucker.

TADPOLE Yeah, they always bloody starve you.
They never give you enough tucker
and you never get enough beer ...

Park chorus (Brian Saaban) in rehearsal, second production, Broome.

Tadpole (Stephen Albert) meets Willie (John Moore), Adelaide.

[*Sleepers roll over in the park, some men and a few women embracing.*]

TADPOLE ... and you never get enough woman either
and that's your trouble.

WILLIE Ah no Uncle I'm good man!

TADPOLE Yeah, I know you, you young bastards!
You fuckin' 'round here, you fuckin' 'round there,
you fuckin' 'round everywhere. Bloody education
that's the thing to get, not this fuckin' 'round.
You wanna end up like your uncle?
Yeah I fuck the sand. I'm here in Perth and I got
fuckin' nowhere to go. What you fuckin' think of this?

WILLIE Yeah, yeah Uncle, I feel sorry now. I don't
know what to tell my mummy!

TADPOLE Never mind I'll fix up your mummy. Come on then.

[*As they go the band plays a few bars reprise of 'A Longway Away from My Country' and those left behind sing softly.*]

ALL *Shake off your burdened delusions,*
Shake off your dreams that weigh down.
You can follow your dreams
But it's not like it seems
Cos your heart will just turn you around ...

TADPOLE We'll go back to Lombadina. I got a lot of things to settle in Broome. Ah you'll find out and they'll find out, when we get there. Anyway what we doing here? C'mon we go.

[WILLIE *and* TADPOLE *downstage sing in duet.*]

WILLIE, TADPOLE
You can follow your dreams
But it's not like it seems
Cos your heart will just turn you around.

A busy city roadside, at traffic lights

[CHORUS *become cars and pedestrians in the city.* WILLIE *and* TADPOLE *make a dive to cross the road. They become separated by cars.* WILLIE *beckons* TADPOLE, *who nearly gets bowled over, which gives him an idea.*]

WILLIE This big place aye Uncle. Big mob motocar.

[*Song: 'Traffic Light'*]

CHORUS *If you stop, stop, stop, stop,*
Bin roaming around in the city
Yoo yoo yoo yoo,
The peak hour traffic just takes its time
Yoo yoo yoo yoo
Confusions controlled in the city
By traffic lights that sure can blind.

Well you start to move,
but can't get very far,
You're lost in a jungle of cars
White gloved cop is waving at you.

[WILLIE *shouts warning to* TADPOLE.]

CHORUS *While all the traffic lights tell you what to do.*

WILLIE Uncle! Quickly now.

CHORUS *See a green light —*

WILLIE Move it.

CHORUS *Yellow light —*

WILLIE Slow down!

CHORUS *Red light —*

WILLIE Uncle —

Chorus (Michael Leslie top) with Willie (John Moore) and Tadpole (Stephen Albert) performing 'Traffic Lights', Adelaide.

CHORUS — *Stop! Don't walk!!*

[*A jammed horn blares.* MARIJUANA ANNIE *and* SLIPPERY *screech to a halt and back up in their car.* MARIJUANA ANNIE *is a hippy in her twenties;* SLIPPERY *is a happy wanderer from Germany in his twenties, on a perpetual high.*]

M. ANNIE — Old man you alright? Yeh?

[TADPOLE *lies in a crumpled heap giving a good impression of a moan.*]

SLIPPERY — Mein Gott! Vhat's happening here?

M. ANNIE — Slippery, come over here and get this old man into the car, we'll take him to hospital.

TADPOLE — Don't you fuckin' take me to hospital,
I don't go to no fuckin' hospital.

M. ANNIE Where do you want to go then?

TADPOLE I wanna go to fuckin' Broome.

M. ANNIE You wanta go to Broome?

TADPOLE Yeah me and this young fella here, we going to fuckin' Broome. You bastards gonna take us there or what?

M. ANNIE It's all right old man, take it easy.

TADPOLE My name Tadpole. Steven Johnson Tadpole.
They call me Tadpole, Uncle Tadpole.

M. ANNIE And who's this one?

TADPOLE Oh! That's Willy.

M. ANNIE Oh Willy!

TADPOLE This my nephew that boy.

M. ANNIE What a spunk!

TADPOLE Oh you don't wanna trust him, that little bastard. Hmph! Willy he bin fuckin' 'round here, he bin fuckin' 'round there, he bin fuckin' 'round everywhere, the little bastard. Well come on, you better help me up, I better jump inside. I wanna fuckin' go to Broome! Him too [*pointing to* WILLIE]. He wanna come to Broome too!

[WILLIE *and* TADPOLE *climb into the 'car.'*]

M. ANNIE Slippery, let's go to Broome, let's take these two blokes to Broome.

SLIPPERY [*Reluctant to take these two 1500 miles overland for free.*]

Ah, ah. I don't know Annie, long way.

[MARIJUANA ANNIE *twists* SLIPPERY *round her finger, turning on the charm and growing wistful at the thought of a tropical paradise.*]

Marijuana Annie (Lynda Nutter), chorus, Slippery (Alan Charlton) and Tadpole (Stephen Albert), Adelaide.

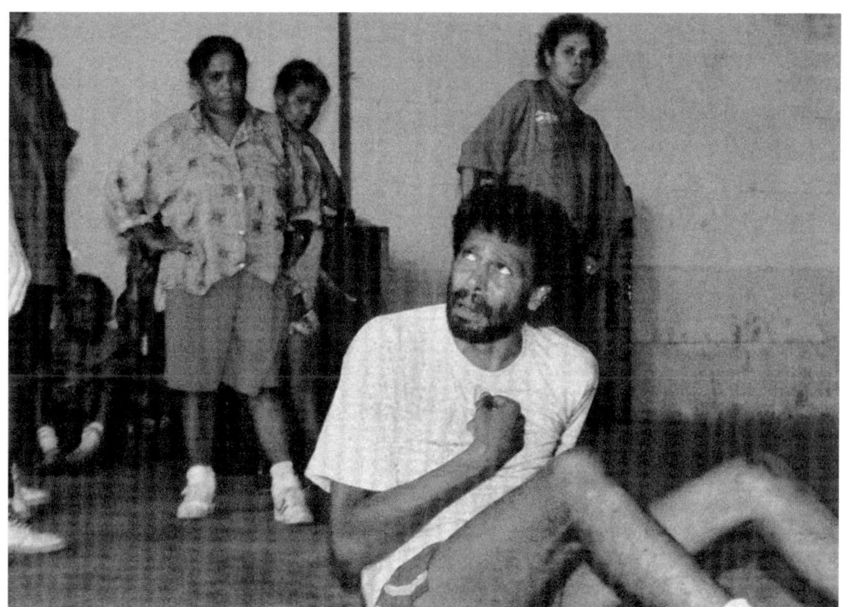

Ernie Dingo as Tadpole with Vanessa Poelina, Sylvia Clarke and Michelle Torres-Hill in rehearsal, first production, Broome.

M. ANNIE — Why not? It's a good place, I hear it's
good out there. Plenty of fishing,
nice beaches and plenty of people
who smoke a little bit of this and that.

SLIPPERY — Is it the same as Yermany?

WILLIE — Ay?

SLIPPERY — Haff they got forests like in Yermany?

M. ANNIE — No they haven't got any forests,
but they got eighty-mile beaches, and reefs and
places you can nestle away in — I think!

[SLIPPERY *is swayed by the thought of passion in the tropics.*]

SLIPPERY — Ah yah I think it is gut to go to Broome. Where you come from old fella, you come from Broome, do you?

TADPOLE — [*Still angry, drunk.*] Yeh, what the fuck, where you come from anyway, you bastard?

SLIPPERY — I come from Yermany, I am escaping the army conscription.

TADPOLE — Who? 'Nother Hitler eh?

Marijuana Annie (Lynda Nutter) and Slippery (Alan Chartton) with chorus (Josephine Lawford), Canberra.

SLIPPERY Ya ya [*Then recollecting himself —*] Nein nein.

M. ANNIE I've heard about this Hitler and all that — he was supposed to have this spear of Longinus, the one that pierced Jesus in the side.

TADPOLE [Real argumentative drunk.] Don't you talk like that about Jesus Christ, he's the saviour — everybody always tells me anyhow — wish the bastard would save us now.

M. ANNIE I'm a Buddhist myself.

TADPOLE Don't you talk about that , that's proper rude thing to say in our language —

WILLIE [*A bit tired of this.*] You mob knocked him over, you goin' take us mob back to Broome or what?

M. ANNIE Come on, Slippery.

[SLIPPERY *gets into the driver's seat next to* TADPOLE. MARIJUANA ANNIE *gets in the back next to* WILLIE *and gives him the eye.*]

SLIPPERY Ah well, I s'pose now that I am in Australia I might as well see it, first hand. And what better experience than to go with you and these two fellows, local people. Aboro-gynal people ... [*he hesitates at the cool stare Tadpole is giving him*]. Coloured people ... native people ... The sort of people that I can relate to in this country, where I am understood, I hope.

[CHORUS *comes down either side of the travellers, miming handline fishing, kuckling, gambling, dreaming, beach relaxing.*]

[*Travel song: 'Feel Like Going Back Home'*]

TADPOLE *Feel like going back home*
Right now while the mangoes are ripe,

Constable Goonganoong (Jimmy Edgar), Sergeant Doogie (Robert Faggetter) performing 'Lay-dy, when you carry this stuff around ...,' Adelaide.

Rohanna Angus, Sylvia Clarke and David Sampi, chorus rehearsal break, Troppo Sound shed, January, Broome.

Frangipanis starting to bloom
And the Bluebone starting to bite.

CHORUS *Hey mum I can just taste your fish soup and rice,*
I'm coming back home to you,
Can't hack the pace of the city life,
Soon I'll be dreaming in Broome.

TADPOLE *The luggers are in on the spring tide*
And the gambling houses are packed.
Banker he mukan with siton
But Larri we got butta in front.

CHORUS *Hey dad we gonna rage a little John Hurt tonight*
Make Orion sing with the moon.
Can't hack the pace of the city life,
Soon I'll be dreaming in Broome.

ALL *Lazy breeze blowin' through your mind,*
Sky blue sea, catch a feed there any time.

[SLIPPERY *and* MARIJUANA ANNIE *pass a smoke around, which* WILLIE *declines.* SLIPPERY *slips into a daze and the car drifts off the road.* TADPOLE *sees the danger just in time.*]

TADPOLE *Feel like going back home*
Right now while the mangoes are ripe,
Jigal tree starting to bloom
And the girrid starting to bite.

CHORUS *Hey mum I can just taste your fish soup and rice,*
I'm coming back home to you,
Can't hack the pace of the city life,
Soon I'll be dreaming in Broome.
Soon I'll be dreaming in Broome.
Soon I'll be dreaming in Broome.

Great Northern Highway, south of Roebourne

M. ANNIE We better stop soon — did you remember to water those plants in the back?

SLIPPERY Ya. But I don't know whether you can keep that stuff here in Australia.

M. ANNIE It's totally necessary Slippery. How do you think I'm supposed to keep my equilibrium and my social outlook together if I don't have this little weed to help me get along?

[*Two khaki-clad northern cops enter and pull them over.*]

COP Pull over there.

M. ANNIE Hey, they're pulling us over —

COP What's this bloody stuff in the back here? Do you realise it's illegal to be in possession of marijew-ahna?

M. ANNIE You can't search our car, you know that's illegal. I've got my rights.

COP Lay-dy, when you carry this stuff around, you've got no rights.

[SLIPPERY *and* MARIJUANA ANNIE *are defiant but* TADPOLE *is used to the situation and influences* WILLIE *to accept it too.*]

M. ANNIE [*As they are hauled off.*] You can't — what are you doing with us? You can't — hey!

COP Jump in. Chuck em in!

WILLIE Oh Chrije — they gonna put us in jail, Uncle.

TADPOLE That's alright — what the fuck I was a lawyer once, I been in jail many times, but I always get out.

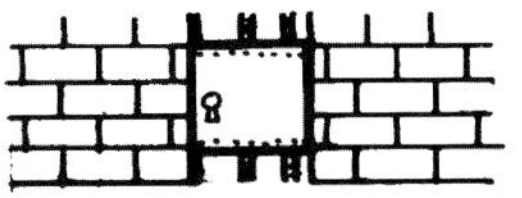

Roebourne Lockup, night

[*The stage darkens, a steel jail door slams shut, keys rattle.* WILLIE, TADPOLE, MARIJUANA ANNIE *and* SLIPPERY *are led to cells.*]

SLIPPERY Who are these people?

[*Song: 'Linjoo Blues'*]

INMATES *Some people call them the cops*
Some people call them police,
Back home in Broome
We call them linjoo.

SLIPPERY [*Protesting.*] I come from Yermany —

COP Where's your passport?

[SLIPPERY *has none.* SERGEANT *grins.*]

SERGEANT What's your name?

SLIPPERY Wolfgang Beutenmuller.

SERGEANT Jesus. How do you spell that?

SLIPPERY B E U T E N M U L L E R — my friends just call me Slippery.

SERGEANT I'm not surprised, Slippery.

INMATES *Smokin' jokin' with my friends —*

WILLIE [*To* MARIJUANA ANNIE.]
That policeman don't like that green stuff
in the back of your car, ay?

INMATES *Got so stoned it was the end —*

COP Listen son, don't get smart with us!

WILLIE Pardon?

INMATES *Someone come and knock on the door —*

SERGEANT Do you realise that you are being charged with possession of marijew-ahna?

COP Now who is responsible for this stuff?

INMATES *Told me not to smoke that gunja no more —*

SLIPPERY Yes they did.

TADPOLE I never seen this stuff before. I don't know what this stuff is.

INMATES *I got the linjoo blues.*

SLIPPERY I don't know — dis feellow who gafe me der car —

INMATES *I got the linjoo blues.*

SLIPPERY Said if you tek dis stuff to Broome ... I'll meet you dere!

INMATES *Stop your foolin', stop your foolin'*
Stop your messing with my head.

M. ANNIE I found it. I'm taking it to Broome for analysis.

INMATES *Stop your foolin', stop your foolin'*
Stop your messing with my head
With my head, with my head.

M. ANNIE I've had enough of this physical harrassment. I know what you police are all about. You just want to lock us all up. Just because we're free spirits and we're trying to have a good time. Everybody wants to lock everybody else up these days. You and me [*to* WILLIE, TADPOLE, *then back to* SERGEANT] well why don't you lock us all up then. Get rid of us!

SERGEANT [*Stares at her.*] Yeah, that's right woman. Done!

[SERGEANT *and* COP *throw* MARIJUANA ANNIE *up and over.*]

Adelaide performance.

Chorus (Vanessa Poelina, David Sampi, Stephen Albert, Della Morrison, Sylvia Clarke), Slippery (Alan Charlton) and M. Annie (Lynda Nutter), Perth.

INMATES *Stop your foolin', stop your foolin'*
Stop your messing with my head.

[SERGEANT *and* COP *do a cakewalk style strut through figures.*]

TADPOLE This your first time in jail, Willie?

WILLIE Yeah uncle, I'm man now.

TADPOLE Never min' my boy ... legal aid get you out of here.

WILLIE Uncle, people die in jail ay?

INMATES *Now I'm sitting down in this cell*
Thinkin' about you baby
Masturbating like hell
Screw come 'round for an early start.

[COP *and* SERGEANT *pounce on* WILLIE.]

COP You come with me feller,
You're here to pull yourself together
Don't pull yourself apart.

INMATES *Stop your foolin', stop your foolin'*
Stop your messing with my head.

[*They belt* WILLIE.]

TADPOLE [*Setting up a commotion.*]
I wanna see the legal aid.
I wanna see the legal aid.

INMATES *Stop your foolin', stop your foolin'*
Stop your messing with my head.

CELL VOICE Steven you old bastard — what they got you for?

TADPOLE This bloke here, he got this ... I don't know, he got plant here, I don't know what kind plant, but they don't like that plant. They chuck us all in. I wanna

'Linjoo Blues,' Perth.

see the legal aid! My brother's the legal aid in this Roebourne town — I'm the cousin brother but really the brother — where's the legal aid?!

CELL VOICE You tell im bro!

TADPOLE Who that?

CELL VOICE I am the legal aid.

TADPOLE Oh fuck im.

INMATES *Stop your foolin', stop your foolin'*
Stop your messing with my head.

TADPOLE Cousin brother! Johnny Johnson!
What they got you in here for?

2nd VOICE Ne' mind. I'll get you all out.
Just tell me what happening.

[*There's a shout of pain —* WILLIE'S *voice.*]

TADPOLE You better listen you bastard — I'll tell you ...

[*Song: 'Listen to the News'*]

[TADPOLE, *then inmates joining in.* WILLIE *leads the dance.*]

TADPOLE *Man of the gun come shot up the son*
and the girl and the child and the mother
but the child is the son and the son is the child
and the child is the son of the father.
And the winds sing the song
of the right and the wrong
and scatters the tunes and the meaning
and the passage of time just follows the line
of the law of the land and the dreaming.

ALL *Listen to the News*
talkin' 'bout the blues
of our people.
Listen to the News
talkin' 'bout the blues
of our people.
Everyday everyday
Discussing a way
Discussing a way.

TADPOLE [*With women inmates, in haunting harmony.*]
The promises made just spelt out the graves
of the living the dead and the dying
for the old and the new
and the words of the few
just knew that the cycle was changing.
For the man of the clock
believed that the lot
of the people were his for the taking
though the law was the same
in his books in his name
in his words which he kept on breaking.

Chorus (Jimmy Edgar, Josephine Lawford), Kalumburu.

Listen to the News
talkin' 'bout the blues
of our people.
Listen to the News
talkin' 'bout the blues
of our people.
Everyday, everyday
Discussing a way
Discussing a way.

CHORUS [*Women of the jail only.*]
In his eyes all are one
all are sons all begun
all fashioned to bend to his reason
and the mother and child
and the father who smiles
on the world as it carries each season.

For all are the same
just born to the name
of the father whose words have been spoken
and the words 'peace on earth'
just carry a curse
when the words are so easily broken.

Listen to the News
talkin' 'bout the blues
of our people.
Listen to the News
talkin' 'bout the blues
of our people.
Everyday, everyday
Discussing a way
Discussing a way.

TADPOLE *But a leader will come*
from the house of the son

Tadpole (Stephen Albert), Kalumburu.

Chorus (Vanessa Poelina), first production, rehearsal, Perth.

and the man and the gun will be broken
and the word will be heard
when the leader is reared
and the words that he speaks
will be spoken.
So look to the day
when the sun shines its rays
cos I know that a new day is dawning
for dawn it will come
when the people as one
shall rise to the light of the morning.

Listen to the News
talkin' 'bout the blues
of our people.
Listen to the News
talkin' 'bout the blues
of our people.

Everyday, everyday
Discussing a way
Discussing a way.

Oo la la la — lalalala — lalalala
Oo la la la la — lalalalala

Oo la la la — lalalala — lalalala
Oo la la la la — lalalalala

Is this the end?
Is this the end of our people?
[*Wail — a woman in the* CHORUS.]
Is this the end?
Is this the end of our people?
[*Wail — a woman in the* CHORUS.]
Is this the end?

Is this the end of our people ?

[*Clapsticks, didgeridoo, darkness.*]

Chorus (Josephine Lawford) and Rosie (Rohanna Angus), Kalumburu.

Bush and pool, Roebuck Plains

[*Birds calling. The travellers wake up by a pool.* SLIPPERY *meditates. A splash of water —* WILLIE'S *head emerges from the pool.* TADPOLE *prowls the scene for bush tucker.*]

M. ANNIE Jesus it's hot.

TADPOLE This Roebuck Plains, this country.

M. ANNIE Fuck is it always this hot up here?

TADPOLE When you come from this country it's not hot. [*Wipes perspiration from his face.*]

M. ANNIE I'm hungry, when do we get to Broome?

[TADPOLE *chases behind the hill and then off stage.*]

SLIPPERY Vat iss he doing?

WILLIE [*Dully.*] Chasing barni.

SLIPPERY Who iss Barney?

WILLIE Bungarra.

SLIPPERY Boong arrow? [***Making** motion of drawing bow.*]

WILLIE Jalangardi.

[SLIPPERY *still perplexed.*]

WILLIE Goanna.

SLIPPERY Why Anna go?

WILLIE BEEEEG LIZARD.

SLIPPERY Big lizard yah? [*Positions hands to length of a small lizard.*]

[WILLIE *spreads his hands out to show an enormous goanna.*]

WILLIE Wah! [*Splashes the water.*]

SLIPPERY [*Scared.*] Verdammte Scheisse!

[*Enter* TADPOLE *and traditional Aboriginal dancers. Females bear bush tucker in bindjins, males have spears and boomerangs.*]

[*Song: 'Jalangardi'*]

TADPOLE *Monsoon clouds are coming,*

FEMALES *Ngarba yunyarri ngarba yunyarri.*

TADPOLE *Gonna bring the Barni too.*

FEMALES *Ngarba yunyarri ngarba yunyarri.*

WILLIE *Magabala Gungkura Gubiny for you*
Going down to Roebuck Plains.

[*Boisterous dance with hunting and food gathering movements.* MARIJUANA ANNIE *is spaced out by it all and entranced by what is happening around her;* SLIPPERY *is frightened of the natives.*]

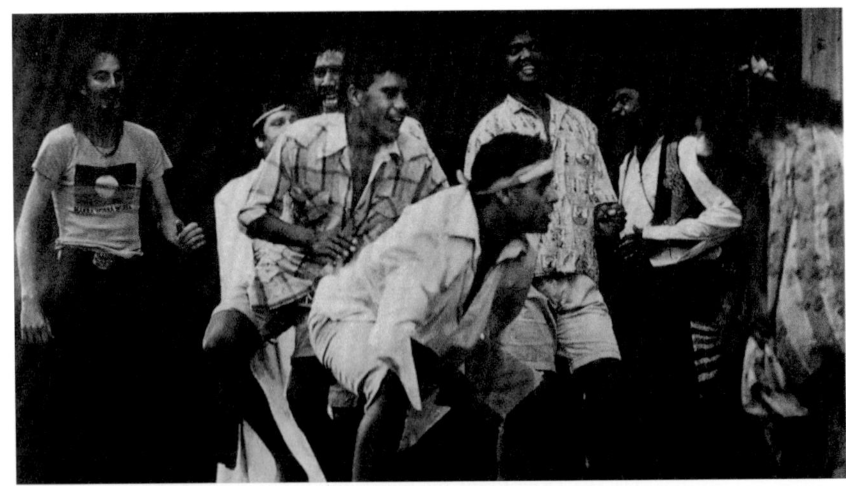

Slippery (Alan Charlton), chorus, Willie (John Moore) and Tadpole (Stephen Albert), Canberra.

Chorus (Ricky Haji Noor) and Willie (John Moore), Canberra.

FEMALES, TADPOLE

Jalangardi, jalangardi
The chase is on
Gotta run, pass im gun
The chase is on.

Karrajarri, Yawuru, Nyikina, Bardi
All running, all running
Must have that mungari, mayi,
And wali and arli, and arli, and arli.

TADPOLE *Because it tastes so good,*
gotta try it sometime.

CHORUS *The chase is on*
Gotta run, pass im gun
The chase is on
Jalangardi, jalangardi.

M. ANNIE Hey this is good.

Rosie (Rohanna Angus), Kalumburu.

Chorus (Michael Leslie, Brian Saaban, Ricky Haji Noor), Broome matinee.

[SLIPPERY *tastes the bush banana and is not impressed; exclaims, spits out.* TADPOLE *leads a song and dance.*]

[*Song: 'Everybody Likes a Magabala'*]

TADPOLE *Everybody likes a lulb'd goanna*
ahha ahha ahha ahha ah-ah

Everybody likes a bush banana
ahha ahha ahha ahha ah-ha

Everybody plucks one
everybody sucks one
everybody's feeling fine.

Everybody knows where
magabala grows yeah
it ripens on the vine, yeah —
it ripens on the vine, yeah —
it ripens on the vine.
Ahha ahha ahha ahha ah-ah

[MARIJUANA ANNIE *and* SLIPPERY *respond to the suggestion of the dance and move up to the hill for lovemaking.* WILLIE *notices them passionately kissing.*]

WILLIE Uncle, what those two doing there?

TADPOLE Wah, you don't look that side.
You mind your own business.

WILLIE No Uncle, look. He grabbing that thing there!

TADPOLE Nobody ever tell you about this kind of thing before?

WILLIE No Uncle, I don't savvy this kind of thing.

TADPOLE No one bin tell you? Well, when man find a woman you gotta make love to them.

WILLIE Eh, Uncle!

Tadpole (Stephen Albert) and Willie (John Moore), Canberra.

TADPOLE I tell you, I tell you — when God made man
[*gestures*] when God made man —
and he made woman [*gestures*].
And he made em different and when they find each
other ... they do that thing. You never ever ... ?
Nobody ever tell you about this kind of thing before?

WILLIE No Uncle.

TADPOLE Well you better go watch 'em.

[MARIJUANA ANNIE *cradles* SLIPPERY *in her arms and sings.* WILLIE *watches.*]

[*Song: 'Afterglow'*]

M. ANNIE *Hush a bye little darlin'*
won't you lay by my side
and we'll fly together
on a celestial ride.
Close your eyes, little darlin'

I love you don't you know?
And we'll bathe together in the afterglow.

I love you little darlin'
I love you oh so much
and I ride on your rhythm
and move with your touch.
Stay awhile little darlin'
oh please please don't go
and we'll bathe together in the afterglow.

Stay awhile little darlin'
stay awhile with your love
keep me safe in your loving
secure in your touch.
Let us just grow together
as loving must grow
and we'll bathe together in the afterglow.

TADPOLE Willie, you got girlfriend?

WILLIE Ay Uncle.

TADPOLE You like woman? This man got woman, you got woman ...

WILLIE Big shame!

TADPOLE [*Pointing with walking stick to* WILLIE'S *lower region.*] You must feel something dere.

WILLIE Uh-Uncle, I got this girl, Rosie ...
[*Confused.*] I like im but I don't know if he like me.
He in Broome now, he bin kicked outta Mission too.
He different one from me ... I don't know if he like me ...

TADPOLE And you wanta be a man or what?
You gonna be stupid man
or you gonna grab im or what?

WILLIE [*Realises acutely his own inadequacy.*]
Ah, I don't know if he like me, Uncle.

TADPOLE You better go and find im and grab im.
You gotta be man now you not baby
anymore — what's wrong with you?!

WILLIE I don't know if he like me, uncle.

TADPOLE Must be proper pretty one, eh?

[*Song: 'If You See Rosie'*]

WILLIE *If you see Rosie*
Won't you tell her that I care;
She's the only one that I love
Won't you tell her I'll be there.
Her hair
all a splendour
as she catch the fire's glow,
that's the Rosie I love
and that you love
I suppose.

[*Women and men watch laughing and join the dance routine.* TADPOLE *sits and watches.*]

If you see her smile
You'll know what I feel
to love and kiss and hold her
would make my life unreal
and for her to say she loves me
would make my life complete ...

TADPOLE *Rosie is the sandwich*
and you want to be the meat!

(Opposite) Tadpole (Ernie Dingo) and chorus (Michael Leslie, David Sampi, Stephen Albert) performing 'Jalangardi', Perth.

Act Two

Chinatown in Broome, outside the Roebuck Bay Hotel

The Roebuck is a legendary bush pub that has seen better days and is trying hard to bring them back. It has big verandahs, for this is the tropics, and a certain tawdry grace. There are no pearling fleets any more, but the jade waters of Roebuck Bay are just across the street. The corrugated iron roofs and shacks of Chinatown are white like a pearl, a dust covered pearl.

[*To the strains of 'Feel Like Going Back Home',* TADPOLE, WILLIE, SLIPPERY *and* MARIJUANA ANNIE *drive into Broome and arrive outside the Roebuck.*]

TADPOLE Hey boy, we're in Broome now.

ALL Yeah!

WILLIE That's the place where I bin used to live before. [*Points.*] Kennedy Hill Reserve up there!

TADPOLE [*Getting his walking stick into action.*] Turn left over there. We better hit the Roebuck I think.

SLIPPERY Vats der Roebuck?

[*Faint music in background — opening bars of 'Time Will Heal.'*]

WILLIE Where all the people drink. Band playing there ...

M. ANNIE Let's get some booze.

TADPOLE That's what you need, everybody needs a drink. If you don't drink you don't shit and if you don't shit, you die!

[*They head for the Branding Iron Bar.*]

Inside the Roebuck — the Branding Iron Bar

[*Couples at tables.* ROSIE, *in white and silver, is the lead singer in a local country and western band. As the travellers enter the bar, the music stops.*]

TADPOLE They real friendly people here.

[*The crowd stares at the new arrivals.*]

[*Song: 'Time Will Heal'*]

ROSIE *I guess that time will heal*
the hurtin' in my heart
but as I contemplate
just how we are apart
I know that I might find
someone to share my life
but I can't understand
the tears I hold inside.

Sometimes I think of you
and wait for someone new
who will engage my dreams
the way you used to do
but now I'm all alone
with memories that I hold
and you are there in these
although you've now grown cold.

[*The music cuts out.* WILLIE *is stunned by* ROSIE'S *appearance — before he faints he sees the crowd as if frozen in time.*]

WILLIE Oh Chrije! That's im, that's the woman
now I bin tell you about! That's im there
now look — he singing ... Ah, I feel funny ...

[WILLIE *swoons back into* TADPOLE'S *arms and sags to the floor.* TADPOLE *revives him with a splash of beer.*]

Chorus (Cecilia Dann, Della Morrison) performing 'Time Will Heal,' Sun Pictures matinee, Broome.

[*Waking up.*] Uncle, I don't like beer on me! You crabhole!

[*Music resumes.*]

TADPOLE Oh don't worry. Come on my boy, you gotta friend him up and try grab im.

[ROSIE *dances with anyone, hasn't noticed* WILLIE *yet.*]

WILLIE But I feel big shame. I'm dirty.

TADPOLE Ah don't worry, we all dirty!

[*He drags* WILLIE *along, heads for* ROSIE.]

ROSIE *Sometimes I think of you*
And wait for someone new
Who will engage my dreams
The way you used to do
But now I'm all alone
With memories that I hold
And you are there in these
Although you've now grown cold.

And you are there in these
Although you've now grown cold.
And you are there in these
Although you've now grown cold.

[*Raucous applause.*]

M. ANNIE [*Tagging along.*] Hey far out!! Wow, wow, this is my kind of scene. Check out the band.

[TADPOLE *fronts* ROSIE *himself.*]

TADPOLE Hullo my girl. My name Tadpole, Steven Johnson Tadpole, Uncle Tadpole, and this one here my boy.

[TADPOLE *feels around for* WILLIE *but he's not there.* ROSIE *reacts to the name.*]

He there at the bar. I think he like you too. I just wanna tell you that I think you singing good, that's good, that's deadly.

ROSIE And what, you wanna have a go old man?
[*Inviting him to dance.*]

TADPOLE Ooh, you give me a go with you?

ROSIE You too old —

TADPOLE Nah! You better let my young boy have a go with you.
I'll have a go at singing. I'll find im this woman.
I'm good singer. I used to sing before in choir.

ROSIE [*To band members.*]
Hey bro! Old man want to get up and play.
Sing us a song, what you reckon?
Give im a go eh?

TADPOLE [*As musicians smile at him and tune up.*]
I wanta sing a country song,
I wanta sing a country song.

[*Band cranks up to a fast country number;* TADPOLE *gets ready to sing and tries to pick up the beat but gets left behind. Crowd claps in time and dances around a bit, ending with a crescendo as* TADPOLE *brings things to a halt by banging his stick.*]

I can't sing a bloody fast song — I'm too old. How can you get a woman singing a fast song. I wanta sing a slow song, real good one like this —

[TADPOLE *taps out the beat with his walking stick, slow and sensual, rocking at the knees. The band starts slower.*]

Yeah, that's im —

[*Whistles and stamps as music warms up.*]

[*Song: 'Is You Mah Baby?'*]

TADPOLE *Is you mah baby, is you mah baby*
is you?

Is you mah baby, is you mah baby
is you?

When I'm in your warm embrace
I feel part of the human race
Oh! ... is you mah baby, is you mah baby
is you?

Is you mah baby, is you mah baby
is you?

Tadpole (Stephen Albert) at the Roebuck with chorus (Della Morrison, Sylvia Clarke), Canberra.

[*During the song he collects the women from the tables. They laugh and whistle and yelp and do a dance routine with him.*]

Is you mah baby, is you mah baby
is you?

You get under mah skin.
Take off your jowidj and let me in
Oh! ... is you mah baby, is you mah baby
is you?

[*Instrumental with dance routine involving whole female cast. Saloon style piano.*]

TADPOLE *Is you mah baby, is you mah baby*
is you?

Is you mah baby, is you mah baby
is you?

You wipe me off my face
let's multiply the Aboriginal race.
Oh is you mah baby, is you mah baby
is you?

Is you mah baby, is you mah baby
is you?

Chorus (Josephine Lawford, Della Morrison, Cecilia Dann, Rasidah Bin Omar) and Tadpole (Stephen Albert), Canberra.

[TADPOLE *is by now surrounded by women.*]

TADPOLE — See, that's how you grab women in this country.

[TADPOLE *looks around for* WILLIE.]

ROSIE — Hello Willie, how are you?

CHORUS — [*Exclaims as they see them together.*]
Ahhhhaahhh. Oooooooh.

ROSIE — You still deadly, Willie.

WILLIE — Thanks, Rosie ...

ROSIE — What time low tide? I'm going for kuckle.
You want to come?

PUBLICAN — Time please, ladies and gentlemen.

[*The crowd reacts, watching them leave together.*]

CHORUS — Ohhhhhhhhhhhhhhhhhhh!

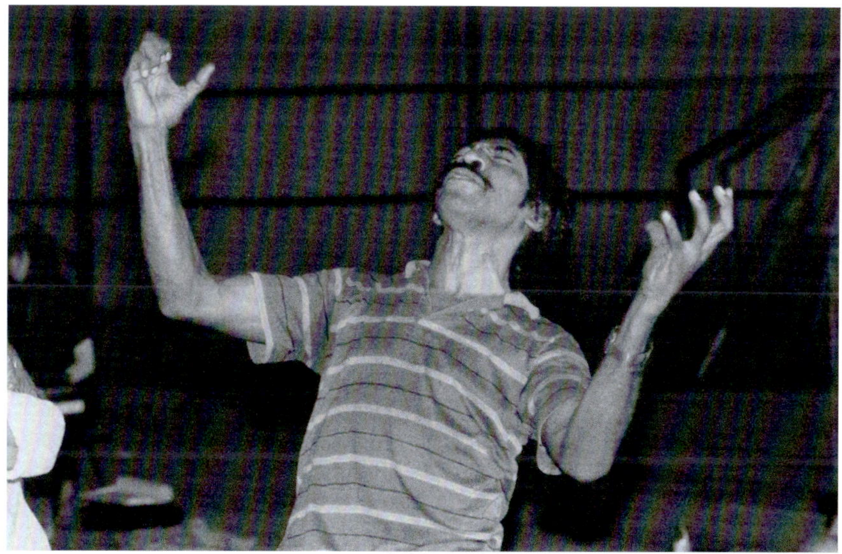

Pastor Flakkon (Jimmy Edgar), second production, rehearsal, Broome.

Down by the mangroves, Roebuck Bay

[*Song: 'Everybody Looking for Kuckle'*]

[ROSIE *dances with* WILLIE, MARIJUANA ANNIE *with* SLIPPERY, TADPOLE *with* CHORUS.]

ALL

OOH OOH-OOH! ... OOH OOH-OOH!
Everybody lookin' for kuckle
everybody lookin' all day
everybody lookin' for kuckle
blackman, whiteman and grey.

Poppa he lookin' for kuckle
poppa he lookin' all day
Mumma bin say he got kuckle
poppa bin sing out hooray.

Everybody lookin' for kuckle — OOH!
everybody startin' to itch — OOH!
everybody lookin' for kuckle — OOH!
everybody mussee jirij — OOH!

Just gip me while you rip me
rip me while you gip me
gip me while you rip me
oh yeah — OOH OOH-OOH! ... OOH OOH-OOH!

WILLIE Hey Rosie.

ROSIE Yeah Willie?

[*Song: 'Nyul Nyul Girl'*]

WILLIE

Nyul Nyul girl, walking out at night,
teeth shining white, nothing else in sight ...
Cos I love you, I'll love you until
there's arrajina Djarindjin hills
arrajina ungarrabin goolil.

Cos I love you, I'll love you until
there's arrajina Djarindjin hills
arrajina ungarrabin goolil.

[*Organ music of the Pentecostal Christians, 'All the Way Jesus', takes over and interrupts* MARIJUANA ANNIE *and* SLIPPERY *in a passionate embrace. They scramble to their feet.*]

[*The Pentecostals enter in procession.* AUNTIE THERESA *and* PASTOR FLAKKON *in white robes.* THERESA *is rapt and does not notice* WILLIE, *who pulls* ROSIE *away behind Kennedy Hill.* TADPOLE *stares at* THERESA, *who hasn't yet seen him.*]

[*Song: 'All the Way Jesus'*]

THERESA and CONGREGATION OF PENTECOSTALS
All the way Jesus, just all the way Lord
Bend me and shape me, give me your reward.
Let me lie in your body, when I'm wracked in my pain
And just light up the loving, that always remains.

Chorus (Della Morrison, et al.), Pastor Flakkon (Stephen Albert), Theresa (Maroochy Barambah) and Slippery (Alan Charlton), Perth.

PR. FLAKKON Tonight is the night of miracles!

WILLIE That my mummy.

PR. FLAKKON Do you believe?

CONGREGATION
We believe!!

WILLIE She don't know I got booted out of school yet.

CONGREGATION
We believe!

WILLIE She think I'm still in Rossmoyne.

PR. FLAKKON Are you Christians?

ROSIE Oh shit —

CONGREGATION
[*Arms upraised.*] Yess!!!

PR. FLAKKON [*Pointing at Tadpole.*] Are YOUUUU Christian?

TADPOLE He's a Christian
I'm a Christian
She's a Christian
We all bloody Christian.

[THERESA *recognises* TADPOLE'S *voice, and is shocked, staring at him.* TADPOLE *slips away.*]

CONGREGATION
Halleluyah!

[*Frenzy in the assembly, possession on the floor and tamborines banging.*]

THERESA Praise the Lord, Halleluyah!

CONGREGATION
Praise the Lord. Halleluyah!

Rosie (Michelle Torres-Hill) and the Roebuck's Branding Iron Bar chorus (Vanessa Poelina, Maroochy Barambah, Della Morrison), Perth.

Chorus (Josie Lawford, Rohanna Angus, Sylvia Clarke) and M. Annie (Lynda Nutter) performing 'Everybody Looking for Kuckle,' Perth.

PR. FLAKKON Tonight is the night when a great weight will be lifted.

CONGREGATION

Amen! Yea! Amen!

PR. FLAKKON And in this hour of darkness a great light will descend upon us and there will indeed be a great revelation.

[WILLIE *watches for a moment in fascination but* ROSIE *draws him aside to slip away during the Pentecostal hymn.*]

THERESA

You may find, if you're true to yourself
That it's all an illusion, the book's on your shelf,
if you read through the lines, then you'll find that it's true
That there's nobody loving like he's loving you.

CONGREGATION

All the way Jesus, just all the way Lord
Bend me and shape me, give me your reward.
Let me lie in your body, when I'm wracked in my pain
And just light up the loving that always remains.

THERESA

Now I know, that it's hard on your soul
When you're down in the gutter, but the story unfolds
How he'll lift you higher, than you've ever been
And he'll show you the glory, that you've never seen.

All the way Jesus, just all the way Lord
Bend me and shape me, give me your reward.
Let me lie in your body when I'm wracked in my pain
And just light up the loving, that always remains.

PR. FLAKKON I can feel someone wants to testify!

M. ANNIE I want, I want to testify. I've been a bad person, I've been bent on sex. I've had a child out of wedlock and I've been using drugs and selling myself to get them and I lost my child. I gave him away after I lost my boyfriend when I was nineteen and he was shot in

Theresa (Sylvia Clarke) and Marijuana Annie (Lynda Nutter), Canberra.

the belly in Vietnam ... aaaaaahh!
And I know I'm not worthy. I'm a sinner and
I'm sorry now — aahhaahhhaahahah.

PR. FLAKKON Sing it one more time for the sister!

CONGREGATION

All the way Jesus, just all the way Lord
Bend me and shape me, give me your reward.
Let me lie in your body, when I'm wracked in my pain
And just light up the loving that always remains.

[SLIPPERY *embraces* MARIJUANA ANNIE. *The* CONGREGATION *gently croons and sways around the two figures huddled together.*]

SLIPPERY Annie, Annie don't worry my dear. I too am evil, I too am a lost indaweeduwal but you haff me now. Things are looking better, we can haff more children, meine Liebe.

Marijuana Annie (Lynda Nutter) and Slippery (Alan Charlton), Perth.

Pastor Flakkon (Stephen Albert), Theresa (Maroochy Barambah), M. Annie (Lynda Nutter) and chorus, Perth.

[*Song: 'Marijuana Annie'*]

SLIPPERY *I know that you're tired and troubled,*
fearful and forlorn,
Tied to your troubles girl that keep on keepin' on
But you know I'll never leave ya
until the morning's dawn,
Marijuana Annie never leave ya
on your own.

CONGREGATION
Marijuana Annie
Blow your blues away
Stop shooting that shot ... gun
Strip the night away.
Marijuana Annie
Blow your blues away
Stop shooting that shot ... gun
Strip the night away.

SLIPPERY *I am tied to troubles too*
That sometimes get me down
I'm tired of trying
As I'm slowly highway bound
But you'll always find some peace
Amongst that hustling highway sound
And to find each other
As the world keeps spinning 'round.

CONGREGATION
Marijuana Annie
Blow your blues away
Stop shooting that shot ... gun
Strip the night away.
Marijuana Annie
Blow your blues away
Stop shooting that shot ... gun

Strip the night away.
Stop shooting that shot ... gun ...

[*Organ holds the last note. The congregation is stirred in sympathy with* MARIJUANA ANNIE. AUNTIE THERESA *comforts her.*]

THERESA My child, my child, we are sisters
of the spirit. I too have lost my child.
I too have been a sinner —

PR. FLAKKON Tonight is the night of miracles,
I told you so, do you believe?

CONGREGATION
We do we do believe —

[AUNTIE THERESA *starts swaying to the music and heaves with her burden of hidden truth as all the women join the movement.*]

[*Song: 'Sweet Sister'*]

THERESA *Life is just a journey, we're tossed from side to side*
You know sweet sister, that you can't be satisfied.

Till you find the answers
hidden in the word
And you find the glory
that lay hidden and unheard.
It's only when you hear and see
the message in your heart
and realise the truth within
that can't be pulled apart.
I know that the searching ends
when you have realised
that the truth remains within
and cannot be denied.

Chorus (Rasidah Bin Omar, Josephine Lawford) and Slippery (Alan Charlton), Kalumburu.

[THERESA *moves from centre stage towards the pool and baptises* MARIJUANA ANNIE. *They walk towards* PASTOR FLAKKON *on Kennedy Hill.*]

CONGREGATION

Wo ho ... sweet sister
See you standing down the line
you've had your troubles
but you've left them all behind
Wo ho ... sweet sister
See you standing down the line
you've had your troubles
but you've left them all behind.

[PASTOR FLAKKON, THERESA *and* MARIJUANA ANNIE *are at the top of Kennedy Hill.*]

THERESA, M. ANNIE

I feel a strange contentment
when you're standing here by me
the boat keeps rocking tossing
turning on the sea.

I can feel the strength within
the fire deep inside
that knowledge keeps you buoyed
against the surging tide.

ALL *Wo ho ... sweet sister*
See you standing down the line
you've had your troubles
but you've left them all behind
Wo ho ... sweet sister
See you standing down the line
you've had your troubles,
but you've left them all behind.

THERESA, M. ANNIE
You've had your troubles ...
but you've left them all behind.

THERESA I had a child too, to another man, to a German missionary. He took my child away and all I had left to console me was alcohol and this photo. Look!

[THERESA *holds up her photo for all to see.*]

CONGREGATION
Benny, oh Benny —

SLIPPERY Mein Vater! Mein Vater!

[SLIPPERY *produces a matching photograph. He and* THERESA *gaze at one another.*]

THERESA My son, my son! [*Reeling from the shock.*]
My prayers have been answered.

SLIPPERY [*Dazed.*] Meine Mutter, meine Mutter —

[*They embrace to a reprise of 'Is You Mah Baby?'*]

SLIPPERY *Ist you my mutti, ist you my mutti?*
Ist you?

Chorus, Tadpole (Stephen Albert), Slippery (Alan Charlton) and Rosie (Rohanna Angus) performing 'Everybody mussee jirij,' Adelaide.

Slippery (Alan Charlton) and chorus performing 'Ich bin ein Aborigine' Perth.

THERESA *Is you my baby, is you my baby,*
Is you?

CHORUS *When I'm in your warm embrace,*
I feel part of the human race,
Oh is you my — mutti/baby,
is you my — mutti/baby,
is you?

PASTOR Hallelujah!
Tonight IS the night! Do you believe?

CONGREGATION
We believe!

TADPOLE [*Entering from the audience.*] Well I got a story to tell if anybody wanna listen. I had a woman. I bin drinkin', I bin drovin' and I bin a Christian. But most of all I bin true to myself. I bin searchin', searchin' for a long time, searchin' for a reason why all this happened and how. Well I come back this time to sort it all out.

I was a young man and I got married and my wife left me. She left me, so I turned to drink, and she had a child to another man. And so I left and I turned to drink and I bin drovin' and drovin' and drovin' and I bin drinkin' and drinkin' and drinkin' and I'm sick of drovin' but I'm not sick of drinkin' ... because that's the woman over there.

[TADPOLE *points to* THERESA.]

THERESA Ooh, Steben, Steben, I never meant to do it. It was the debbil's work. Steben wait for me!

[TADPOLE *storms downstage, off the stage and up the aisles, followed by* THERESA.]

SLIPPERY Mutti, my mutti wait for me. First I yam Cherman, and den I find that my mutti is Aborigine. Now she iss leaving me again. Und I vunder vhy?

CONGREGATION

[*Looming over him.*] Because we're all born black!

PR. FLAKKON Go with them my children. Seek ye first the kingdom of heaven and it shall be all added unto you! The Lord be praised —

CONGREGATION

Praise the Lord!

SLIPPERY Ich bin ein Aborigine!!

[SLIPPERY *and* MARIJUANA ANNIE *run forward, offstage and up the aisles. The* CONGREGATION *becomes a* CHORUS *again.* ROSIE *emerges from their hiding place and runs onto the stage, with* WILLIE *in pursuit.*]

WILLIE Hey Rosie, wait —

ROSIE Willie?

Chorus (Brian Saaban, Michael Leslie) and Rosie (Rohanna Angus) performing 'Bran Nue Dae' Canberra.

[*Song: 'Djarindjin Girl'*]

WILLIE *Be my Djarindjin girl*
Be the one that I dream of
Be my Djarindjin girl
Be the one that I love.

Don't you ever despair
I won't let you down
Be my Djarindjin girl
Lost but now you're found.

I wait late in the night
Waiting and dreaming of you — boy
You come and lay by my side
Making my dreams all come true.

[WILLIE *and* ROSIE *walk arm in arm to the top of the hill, about to kiss —*]

CHORUS Ooooohhh — (whistle, hoot)

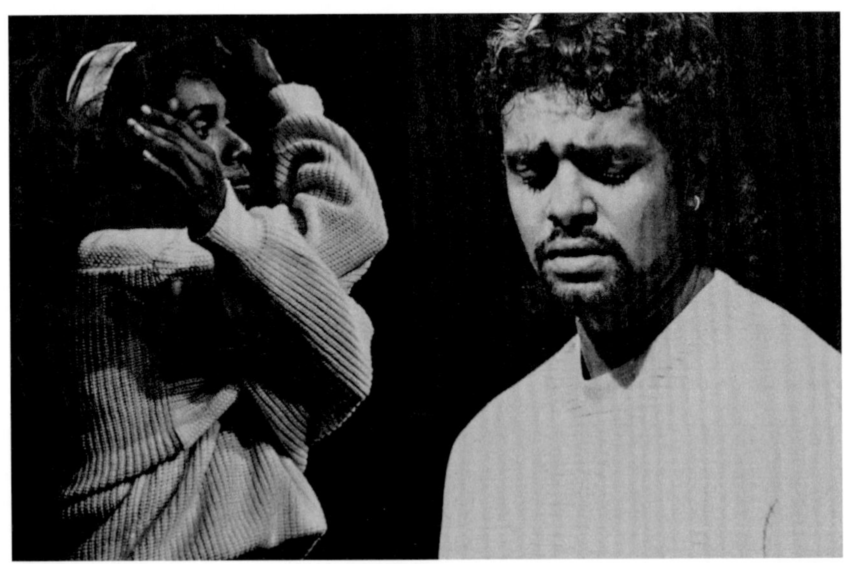

Cecilia Dann, chorus. John Moore, Willie.

[WILLIE *and* ROSIE *become aware of the* CHORUS *and the audience, and scramble embarrassed behind the hill. The female* CHORUS *sits on the deck chairs of Sun Pictures. The male* CHORUS *advances on their counterparts with a proposal. The girls flirt back, leaving their deck chairs.*]

[*Song: 'Seeds That You Might Sow'*]

BOYS *She was only sixteen*
just a child upon the road
when I moved up to her slowly
said, I got a heavy load.
She says

GIRLS *Maybe, come on baby*
would you like to come on down
and we'd rock and reel and reel and rock
all over Chinatown.

ALL *She says hey boy*
Don't you really go
I don't feel so mad about the seeds
that you might sow.
She says hey boy
Don't you really go
I don't feel so mad about the seeds
that you might sow.

BOYS *Well I moved up to her slowly*
and I asked her for a go
and she spoke to me quite softly
in a voice so sweet and low.
She said —

GIRLS *Well I like polony or perhaps a sausage roll*
but if you don't use those condoms
then you cannot pook my hole.

ALL *She says hey boy*
Don't you really go
I don't feel so mad about the seeds
that you might sow.

She says hey boy
Don't you really go
I don't feel so mad about the seeds
that you might sow.

BOYS *Well I am so happy cos I did*
what I was told
for I used those frangers
and she let me pook her hole.

ALL *She says hey boy*
Don't you really go
I don't feel so mad about the seeds
that you might sow.
She says hey boy

Chorus (Brian Saaban, Michael Leslie) and Rosie (Rohanna Angus) performing 'Bran Nue Dae' Canberra.

Theresa and Willie (Sylvia Clarke, John Moore), Canberra.

Don't you really go
I don't feel so mad about the seeds
that you might sow.

[CHORUS *exits stage right, casting condoms into the audience.* TADPOLE *and* THERESA *enter, followed by* MARIJUANA ANNIE *and* SLIPPERY, *who is dressed in Land Rights gear.* THERESA'S *pure white gown is astray. So is her hair.*]

THERESA — Steben, Steben — wait for me!

TADPOLE — I'm going back all the way
to Lombadina when I find that boy!

THERESA — So am I, Steben, with you. What 'that boy'?

TADPOLE — I'm a tracker, I find im — up there ...

SLIPPERY — Yeah Uncle Tadpole Vater wait for me —

TADPOLE — I'm not your fada, that mission fella
[*with emphasis*] your fada!

Kennedy Hill

[TADPOLE *climbs Kennedy Hill and* WILLIE *stands up.*]

WILLIE — [*Smiling, naked.*] Uncle — I'm a man now.

[*Shocked at seeing* WILLIE *as nature made him.*]

THERESA — Willie! Cover yourself up. I don't want to see you naked.

TADPOLE — And I don't want to see your noora.

M. ANNIE — What have you two been up to then, eh?

SLIPPERY — Making da boom boom.

THERESA — Whadda yow — you bella bin coming to us smelling rude yow —

WILLIE — [*Coming down with* ROSIE.] I'm in heben.
That what they tell me when you go to church.
I neber believe them before.

TADPOLE — Poo — you bella stink, go wash your lagurr.

THERESA — Stop that William, stop talking like that.
Why aren't you in school, in Rossmoyne!?
Where's you school uniform I scraped and saved for?

WILLIE — Mum — [TADPOLE *is thunderstruck.*] — you been like this ever since I was young. I can't be like you, I don't wanna be like you, I can't handle you. You mix me up all the time so I don't know if I'm black or white or yellow or green or rainbow warrior! And I don't think you know what you are either.

THERESA — My son ...

TADPOLE — Your son?

THERESA And your son!

[TADPOLE *stares at her, then at* WILLIE, *beginning to smile.*]

TADPOLE Boy, you my son — I know ... I can feel im — but how come is my son?

THERESA That time you come to me, before you go ...

WILLIE Daddy —

SLIPPERY Brother —

[*Reprise: 'Is You Mah Baby?' They sing variations.*]

WILLIE, SLIPPERY, TADPOLE, THERESA [*Embracing.*]

Is you my brother/baby, is you my brother/baby,
is you?
Is you my daddy, is you my daddy,
is you?

You wipe me offa my face,
let's multiply the Aboriginal Race,
oh is you my brother/baby, is you my father/baby,
is you?

[THERESA *stands in the midst of the rejoicing.*]

TADPOLE I been drovin' I been drinkin'
I bin Christian I bin everything
and now I seen everything
and now it's time I gotta go home
see old people ...

[THERESA *begins to cry at the resolution of her past mistakes.*]

[*Song: 'Town by the Bay'*]

TADPOLE *Why are you crying, my pretty Colleen?*
Why are your eyes filled with tears?

Let me come over and dry your eyes
and tell you the way that I feel.

THERESA, TADPOLE

Closer come closer, don't throw me away.
I am so tired and so blue.
I'm dreaming of someone so far far away —
[*To* TADPOLE.] *and sharing these memories with you.*

[CHORUS *enters bearing small boats with lighted candles. They represent the many races of Broome. Finally, they launch the boats on the water.*]

ALL *Just one step closer, don't throw me away*
and carry me back to my town by the bay.
When the darkness is falling at passing of days
won't you cherish the memory of my town by the bay?

THERESA *I still remember the old mission yards,*
the old days the old ways, the times that were hard,
the friends of my childhood, when I was young,
the fathers the brothers, the old Irish nuns —

ALL *So just come one step closer, don't throw me away*
and carry me back to my town by the bay.
When the darkness is falling at passing of days,
won't you share your new future in my town by the bay?

When the darkness is falling at passing of days,
won't you share your new future in my town by the bay?

TADPOLE Come on, we gotta go to Lombadina now, come on you old mob, this not our country. Our country up there. Come on you young bastards, you gotta come with us too. We family now. Willie — Rosie!

[*To the strains of 'Nothing I Would Rather Be',* MARIJUANA ANNIE, SLIPPERY, TADPOLE, THERESA, WILLIE *and* ROSIE *all jump in the car and set off.*]

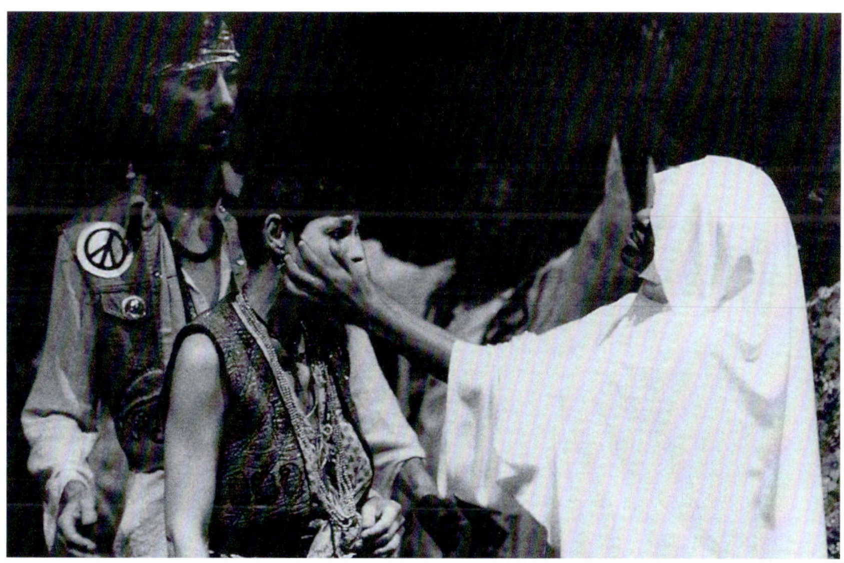

Slippery (Alan Charlton), M. Annie (Lynda Nutter) and Theresa (Maroochy Barambah), Perth.

[MARIJUANA ANNIE *puts her hand up.*
SLIPPERY *stops the car and they all look at her.*]

M. ANNIE

I got 'nother confession to make —
I too am one of you. I was adopted out
as a child — all I can remember is being taken
from a sea of wailing black faces and being raised
in the city, to be white ... I too am an Aborigine!

[CHORUS *celebrates with cries.*
Reprise of 'Nothing I Would Rather Be.']

ALL

There's nothing I would rather be
than to be an Aborigine,
and watch you take my precious land away,
oh no no no —
And watch you take my precious land away!
Ohhhhhh no.

[*Ethereal music, strains of 'Child of Glory.' The car stops again.*]

Tadpole (Stephen Albert) and chorus, Kalumburu.

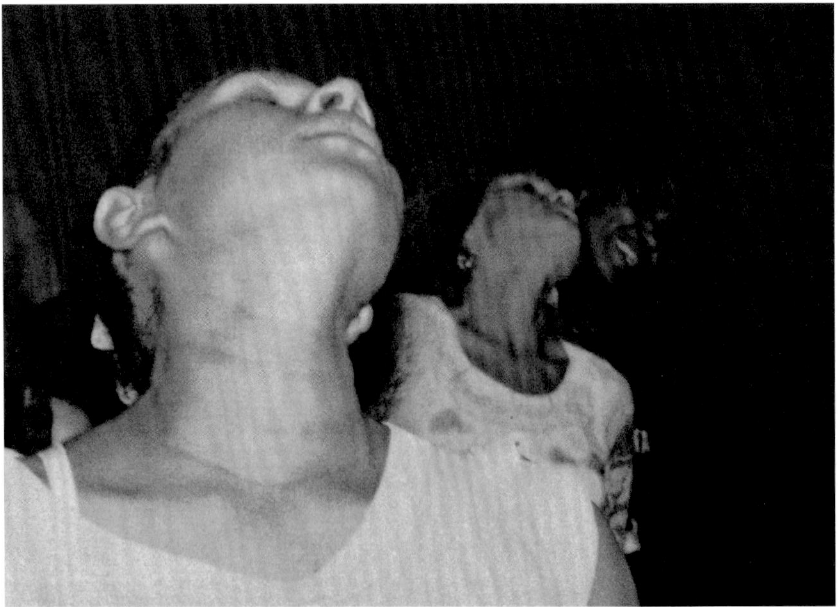

Theresa (Michelle Torres-Hill) and chorus (Della Morrison, Josie Lawford), first production, rehearsal, Broome.

Djarindjin–Lombadina

TADPOLE There him, there hi. There Djarindjin hills.

M. ANNIE Hey, we're in Lombadina.

SLIPPERY Wahhh — it's just like Goa.

[CHORUS *carries on stage a statue of the Christ child in a bindjin followed by the church in the form of a frame, topped with a cross with garlands of flowers.*]

M. ANNIE What's happening?

TADPOLE Ahh — feast of Christ the King! Our anniversary, Th'resa.

THERESA Waddow 'teben!

TADPOLE Porbella porbella. We hhhhome now.

WILLIE, ROSIE [*Speaking fast, moved by the occasion.*] Let's join procession, let's join procession.

[MARIJUANA ANNIE *and* SLIPPERY *stare in amazement at the procession and are drawn by the stately movement. They move to join the slowly measured procession of Christ the King.*]

[*Song: 'Child of Glory'*]

ALL *Child of glory come take me by the hand,*
help me, heal me, and make me understand.
All I survey is there at your command,
Child of glory come take me by the hand.

Though the journey is tortured and so long,
it's the same path the Christ child trod upon.
Child of glory come take me by the hand help me,
heal me and make me understand.

'Child of Glory', Adelaide Festival Centre.

[*The Djarindjin–Lombadina community greets the new arrivals.* THERESA *is silent.* BENEDICTUS *appears from within the framework of the church.*]

BENEDICTUS Velcome, velcome my long lost children.

WILLIE Oh Crije, Benny!

THERESA [*To* SLIPPERY.] That's your father

SLIPPERY Mein Gott im Himmel — mein Vater!

TADPOLE And I'm your father 'nother way.

[BENEDICTUS *covers his embarrassment with a handy diversion.*]

BENEDICTUS Villie! Der prodigal son —
Ah Rosie ... und Tadspole, und Theresa.

SLIPPERY Und Slippery.

M. ANNIE Und Annie.

BENEDICTUS Slippery?

THERESA Father, this is Wolfgang.

BENEDICTUS Wolfgang, mein Sohn. Ah Wolfgang Amadeus Beutenmuller.

[*They break into the chorus of 'Is You Mah Baby?' in German.*]

WILLY [*Cheeky drawl.*] Fa-ada!

BENEDICTUS Ah Villie. Und Slippery und Annie — Ve are all fallen angels and ve all haff a multitude of crosses to bear. You haff kom back, und I haff kom back! Ze mission is finished! Der Auftrag ist zu Ende.

[THERESA *is very still. Everybody lets out one great sigh, a mixture of regret and relief.*]

BENEDICTUS Ve are all angels und devils
Creatures of darkness and bodies of light ...
Lux in tenebris!

TADPOLE What that, toilet soap?

BENEDICTUS Dere is no beginning and dere is no end
in our long journey through life ...

TADPOLE That's what I been tryin' to tell you mob
from the beginning, I been drovin'
I been drinkin', I been drovin' and
drinkin' and drovin' and anyway ...

[*Song: 'Bran Nue Dae'*]

TADPOLE [*Recitative*] *This fella song all about the Aboriginal people, coloured people, black people longa Australia. Us people want our land back, we want im rights, we want im fair deal, all same longa white man. Now this fella longa Canberra, he bin talkin' about a Bran Nue Dae — us people bin waiting for dijwun for 200 years now. Don' know how much longer we gotta wait, and boy it's makin' me slack.*

[*Sings.*] *Here I live in this tin shack*
Nothing here worth coming back
To drunken fights and awful sights
People drunk most every night.

CHORUS *On the way to a Bran Nue Dae*
Everybody everybody say
On the way to a Bran Nue Dae
Everybody everybody say.

TADPOLE [*Recitative.*] *Other day I bin longa to social security, I bin ask longa job — they bin say, 'Hey, what's your work experience?' I bin tell im, 'I got nothing.' They say, 'How come?' I say, ''Cause I can't find a job.'*

Tadpole (Emie Dingo), Theresa (Maroochy Barambah), Rosie (Michelle Torres-Hill) and Willie (John Moore), Perth.

Willie (John Moore) and chorus performing 'In His eyes all are one — Listen to the News,' Adelaide.

Chorus performing 'On the way to a Bran Nue Dae,' Perth.

TADPOLE *We've nothing old, and nothing new*
want us all to be like you,
We've no future we have no past
Hope the sun will shine at last.

CHORUS *On the way to a Bran Nue Dae*
Everybody everybody say
On the way to a Bran Nue Dae
Everybody everybody say.

BENEDICTUS Ve are all sinners, mein children,
but I haffvun leedle reward for der prodigal son —

[BENEDICTUS *throws back the screen of the church to reveal a huge fridge. The door swings open and the glowing interior is filled with stacked red wrapped confections — Cherry Ripe bars, which* BENEDICTUS *begins handing out with abandon.*]

WILLIE Cherry Ripe bro!

BENEDICTUS Line up, meine children!
I like im too —

ALL *On the way to a Bran Nue Dae*
Everybody everybody say
On the way to a Bran Nue Dae
Everybody everybody say.

[CHORUS *throws Cherry Ripes into the audience.* BENEDICTUS *remains on the upper level, arms outstretched in blessing.*]

TADPOLE [*Recitative*] *They bin talk about this kind, that kind, anykind, everykind, but still same kind — and boy make me slack —*

CHORUS *Bran Nue Dae. Ooohhh!!!*

[BENEDICTUS *describes a crucifix, performing a blessing with two Cherry Ripe bars held up as a cross, to absolve all present from their sins of omission.*]

Benedictus (Robert Faggetter), Tadpole (Stephen Albert), Theresa (Sylvia Clarke) and chorus, Adelaide.

BENEDICTUS Absolvo Te.

[*The cast assembles as in a portrait, with the various couples paired:* ROSIE/WILLIE, TADPOLE/THERESA, MARIJUANA ANNIE/SLIPPERY.]

[*Song: 'If I Gave My Heart To You'*]

ROSIE, WILLIE *If I gave my heart to you*
would you promise to be true
it would break my heart in two
if you left me waiting, anticipating.

THERESA, TADPOLE
That some other magic day
I may steal your heart away
but till then I hope and pray
that my love will break through
and in time just move you.

M. ANNIE, SLIPPERY
To a world of different dreams
where all things aren't what they seem
and then you will take my hand
and understand me, when you really see me.

ALL *For only truth remains*
for all things are just the same
for accepting's part of truth
when I give my heart,
when I gave my heart
when I give my heart to you.

[*The cast goes up to heaven, singing 'Bran Nue Dae.'*]

(Opposite) Rosie (Rohanna Angus) and Willie (John Moore), Adelaide Festival Centre.

Bran Nue Dae Music

Songs in the order of performance,
with composers and lyricists

LIGHT A LIGHT

Words and music by James Chi

CALLING IN THE NAME

Words and music by James Chi

NOTHING I WOULD RATHER BE

Words and music by James Chi

A LONGWAY AWAY FROM MY COUNTRY

Words and music by James Chi

TRAFFIC LIGHTS

Words and music by James Chi, Patrick Bin Amat, Garry Gower, Michael Manolis, Stephen Pigram

E D E D E
D E D B7
SEE A GREEN LIGHT
B7
YEL - LOW LIGHT RED LIGHT STOP!
Bm SOLO
Bm A
D.S.

FEEL LIKE GOING BACK HOME

Words and music by Stephen Pigram

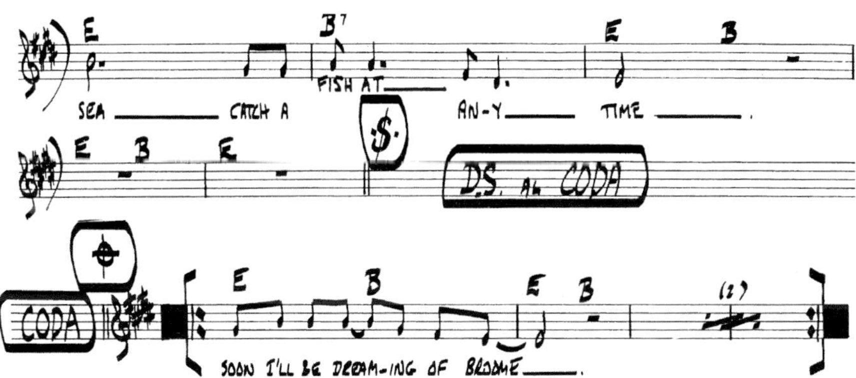

Amhem Hunter, and tour percussionist, second production.

LINJOO BLUES

Words and music by Michael Manolis

B7
STOP YOUR MESS-ING WITH MY HEAD
1. E E6 E E6 E E6
E E6 E E6 E E6
E SOLO
D C#m B
C#m7
STOP YOUR FOOL-ING. F#m STOP YOUR FOOL-ING.
B7
STOP YOUR MESS-ING WITH MY HEAD.
E E6 E E6
E E6 E E6
TILL READY
E E6 E E6
NOW I'M SIT-TING DOWN IN MY CELL YEAH.
E E6 E E6 E E6 E E6
THINK-ING 'BOUT YOU BA-BY MAS-TER-BAT-ING LIKE HELL.
E E6 E E6 E E6 E E6
SCREW COME ROUND FOR AN EAR-LY START.
E7(-10)
"LISTEN HERE BOY YOU'RE HERE TO PULL YOURSELF TOGETHER. DON'T PULL YOURSELF APART."
D.S.

LISTEN TO THE NEWS

Words and music by James Chi, Garry Gower, Michael Manolis

Stephen Pigram, musical director, lead guitarist and former Kuckles band member, first production.

EVERYBODY LIKES A MAGABALA

Words and music by James Chi

AFTERGLOW

Words and music by James Chi

IF YOU SEE ROSIE

Words and music by James Chi

BALLAD

TIME WILL HEAL

Words and music by James Chi

IS YOU MAH BABY?

Words and music by James Chi

EVERYBODY LOOKING FOR KUCKLE

Words and music by James Chi, Patrick Bin Amat, Garry Gower, Michael Manolis and Stephen Pigram

E A E A
EV'-RY BO — DY LOOK-ING FOR — KUC-KLE —.
E A E A
EV'-RY BO — DY MUS-SEE PLAY — PLAY —.
B C
GIP ME WHILE YOU RIP ME —. RIP ME WHILE YOU GIP ME —.
D E
GIP ME WHILE YOU RIP ME. OH — YEAH —.
E A
SOLO TILL READY
D.S. AL CODA
CODA
E A E A
POP-PA — HE LOOK-ING FOR — KUC-KLE —.
E A E A
POP-PA — HE LOOK-ING ALL — DAY —.
E A E A
MOM-MA BIN — SAY HE GOT — KUC-KLE —.
E A E A
POP-PA — BIN SING OUT HOO — RAY —.
B C
GIP ME WHILE YOU RIP ME —. RIP ME WHILE YOU GIP ME —.
D E
GIP ME WHILE YOU RIP ME OH — YEAH —.
fine

ALL THE WAY JESUS

Words and music by James Chi

MARIJUANA ANNIE

Words and music by James Chi, Patrick Bin Amat,
Garry Gower, Michael Manolis, Stephen Pigram

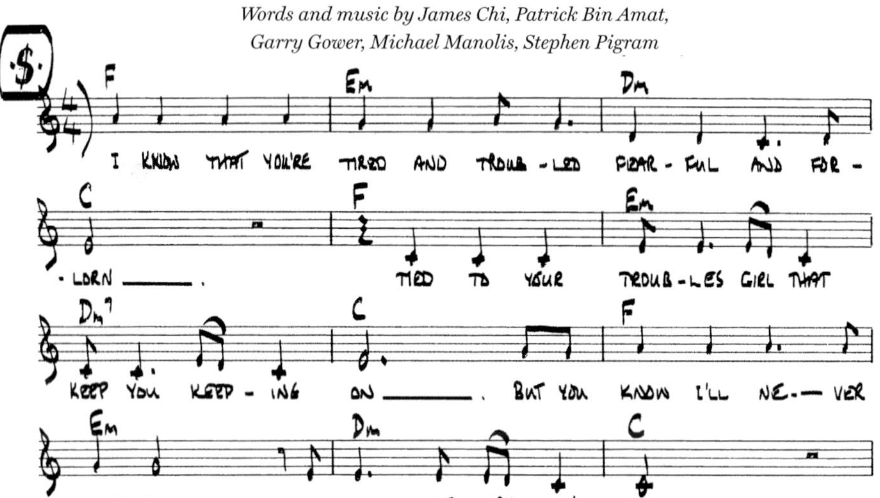

Mick Manolis, musical director, second production, tour and former Kuckles band member; Patrick Bin Amat, both productions, tour and former Kuckles band member.

F Em Dm
MAR-I-JUAN-A AN-NIE ___. NE-VER LEAVE YOU ON YOUR
C F G
OWN ___. MA-RI-JUAN-A AN ___ NIE ___.
F C
BLOW YOUR BLUES ___ A-WAY ___. STOP SHOOT-ING THAT
F G F 1. C
SHOT ___ GUN ___ STRIP THE NIGHT A-WAY ___
2. C
MAR-I-JUANA-A WAY ___ WHEN YOU'RE DOWN AND
F Em Dm C
TROU ___ BLED ___ AND TIMES GET HARD ___.
C F Em Dm
KEEP ON BE ___ LIEV ___ ING ___. AND MAKE A
C F Em Dm
START ___ FOR THE DAWN IS BREAK ___ ING ___ AND I'LL BE
C F G
THERE ___. I'LL AL-WAYS LOVE ___ YOU ___
Dm C
I'LL AL-WAYS CARE ___. MAR-I-JUAN-A

AN NIE BLOW YOUR BLUES A - WAY.
STOP SHOOT-ING THAT SHOT GUN STRIP THE NIGHT A -
1. - WAY MAR-I-JUAN-A
2. WAY
D.S. AL CODA
CODA
I AM TIED TO TROU-BLES TO THAT
SOME-TIMES GET ME DOWN. I'M TIRED OF
TRY-ING AS I'M SLOW- -LY HIGH-WAY BOUND. BUT YOU'LL
AL-WAYS FIND SOME PEACE ON EARTH THAT HUST-LING HIGH-WAY
SOUND. AND TO FIND EACH O-THER AS THE
WORLD KEEPS SPIN-NING 'ROUND. MAR-I-JUAN-A etc....

O SWEET SISTER

Words and music by James Chi

Garry Gower, Kuckles band member, 1978.

SEEDS THAT YOU MIGHT SOW

Words and music by James Chi, Patrick Bin Amat,
Garry Gower, Michael Manolis, Stephen Pigram

TOWN BY THE BAY

Words and music by James Chi

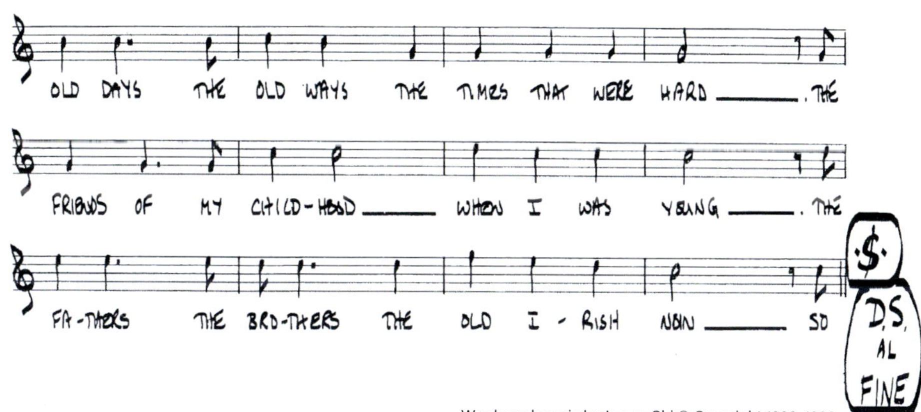

Johnny Sahanna, lead and rhythm guitar, second production and tour.

BRAN NUE DAE

Words and music by James Chi and Michael Manolis

IF I GAVE MY HEART

Words and music by James Chi

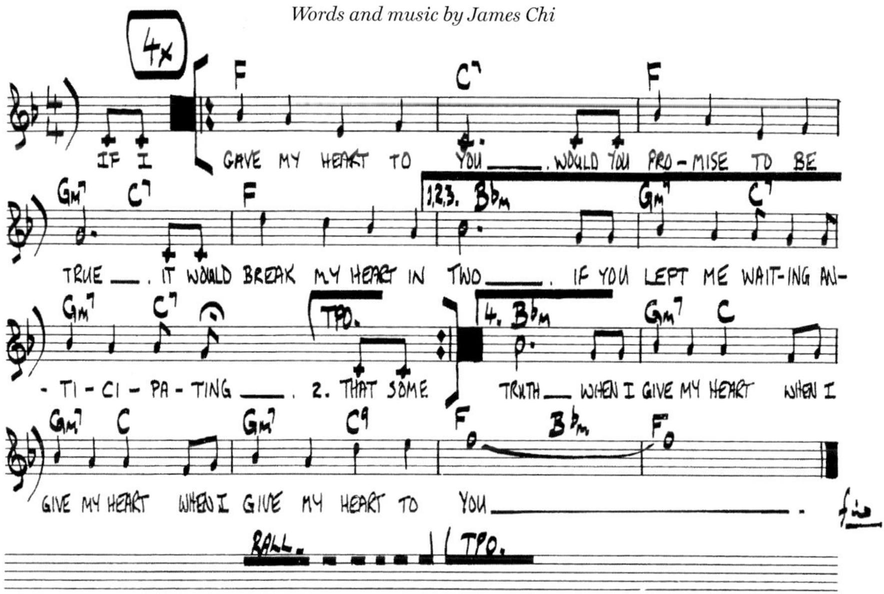

Language

Broome Kriol and Aboriginal language as used in the play

arli	fish
arrajina	nothing
ay	ay, isn't that so, as in 'Ay bro?'
Bardi	language group on the Dampier Peninsula
barni	large goanna
bindjin	coolamon, large wooden carrying dish
butta	second best hand, kudja kudja, gambling game with sticks
dijwun	this one
Djarindjin	site of Lombadina mission
girrid	a food fish. also 'snapper'
goolil	turtle
gunja	marijuana
gungkura	a fruit, bush food
gubiny	a fruit, bush food
he	interchangeably he or she
jalangardi	goanna
jigal	Bauhinia tree
jirij	ejaculate, move suddenly
jowidj	pants
Karajarri	language group
kuckle	cockle
lagurr	eggs or testicles
linjoo	police
Lombadina	mission: Djarindjin
lulb'd	roasted in the earth
mayi	bush food from plants
magabala	a vine fruit, bush food
mukan	food, Malay word
munga	just like, same as
mungari	food
mussee	must
ngarba	water
noora	posterior
Nyikina	language group
pook	poke
siton	highest hand in kudja kudja
stalebait	fishing term, for people
tonguing	longing
ungarrabin	young green turtle
wali	meat
Yawuru	language group
yunyarri	coming

Acknowledgements

(as they appeared in the first edition of *Bran Nue Dae*)

The printing of this book was made possible by generous assistance from Wim Wenders Film Produktion; the Manager, Cadjebut Joint Venture; BHP Minerals Ltd; Hon Ernie Bridge JP MLA, Minister for the North West; Marra Worra Worra Aboriginal Corporation; the Australian Freedom from Hunger Campaign; Chinatown Music and Linneys, Broome; Hon Tom Stephens MLC; Djarindjin Aboriginal Community.

Special thanks to Marita Darcy for assistance in the development of the script, Garry Gower and Steve Pigram, and to Duncan Campbell for the musical arrangements. Thanks to Peter Bibby and Andrew Ross (for further work on the script), Jack Davis, Mudrooroo Narogin, Peter Yu, Richard Walley, Chris McGuigan, Marion Granich, Peter Strain, Phil Thompson, Maria Mann, Robert Juniper, Ernie Dingo, Brian Syron and ANTT, Robyn Kershaw, Duncan Ord and the WA Theatre Company. Thanks also to the Aboriginal Arts Unit of the Australia Council, Aboriginal and Torres Strait Islander Commission, Ansett WA, Cable Beach Club, Sun Pictures, Magabala Books, and Broome Musicians Aboriginal Corporation.

JC

Photographic credits

Lorrie Gratan: pps 3, 5, 6, 17, 18, 26 (both), 38, 42–3, 46, 55–6, 63, 71, 72 (left), 74–5, 87, 115, 116 (right). **David Wilson:** pps 9 (lower), 14, 20 (lower), 23–5 (upper), 28 (upper), 33 (upper), 69 (upper), 82–5 (lower), 88. **Peter Bibby:** pps ix (upper, middle), x–xi, 9 (upper), 11, 20 (upper), 25 (lower), 28 (lower), 37, 38, 40, 44 (upper), 57, 61 (upper), 67, 80 (upper), 99, 107, 116 (left). **Michael Hughes:** pps ix (lower), 44 (lower), 52. **Don Brice:** front cover. [Photographer not known: pps vii, 104, 110.] **Stephen Smith:** pps ii, iii, v, x (lower), xii, 13, 28 (lower), 33 (lower), 35, 39, 49, 59, 61 (lower), 64 (upper, lower), 69 (lower), 72 (right), 79, 80 (lower), 85 (upper), 86.

This edition published 2025
First published 1991
Reprinted 1996, 1999, 2003 by Currency Press Pty Ltd, Paddington NSW, and
Magabala Books Aboriginal Corporation, Broome, WA.
Magabala Books acknowledges the partnership with Currency Press Pty Ltd for previous editions of this book.

Magabala Books Aboriginal Corporation
1 Bagot Street, Broome, Western Australia
Website: www.magabala.com Email: sales@magabala.com

Magabala Books is assisted by the Australian Government through Creative Australia, its principal arts investment and advisory body. The State of Western Australia has made an investment in this project through the Department of Local Government, Sport and Cultural Industries.
Magabala Books acknowledges the generous support of private donors through the Magabala Books Cultural Fund, including the Jon & Caro Stewart Family Foundation and the Spinifex Trust.

Magabala Books is Australia's leading independent Aboriginal and Torres Strait Islander publishing house. We acknowledge the Traditional Owners of the Country on which we live and work. We recognise the unbroken connection to traditional lands, waters and cultures. Through what we publish, we honour all our Elders, peoples and stories, past, present and into our collective futures.

Typeset by Post Pre-Press Group
Printed in China by C&C Offset Printing Co., Ltd.
ISBN 9781925936384 (print) 9781922864024 (ebook)

A catalogue record for this book is available from the National Library of Australia

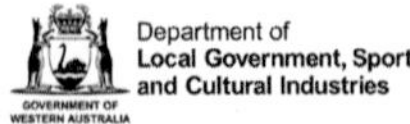